LEISURE GUIDE

South Downs
& Coast

GW00697269

Authors: Tim and Anne Locke
Verifier: Tim Locke
Managing Editor: David Popey
Project Management: Bookwork Creative Associates Ltd
Designers: Liz Baldin of Bookwork Creative Associates Ltd and Andrew Milne
Picture Library Manager: Ian Little
Picture Research: Liz Allen, Alice Earle, Carol Walker and Vivien Little
Cartography provided by the Mapping Services Department of AA Publishing
Copy Editors: Marilynne Lanng of Bookwork and Pam Stagg
Internal Repro and Image Manipulation: Sarah Montgomery
Production: Rachel Davis

Produced by AA Publishing
© AA Media Limited 2007
Reprinted 2007
Updated and revised 2010

Published by AA Publishing (a trading name of AA Media Limited, whose registered office is Fanum House, Basing View, Basingstoke, Hampshire RG21 4EA; registered number 06112600).

ISBN 978-0-7495-6694-4
ISBN 978-0-7495-6707-1(SS)

A CIP catalogue record for this book is available from the British Library.

The contents of this book are believed correct at the time of printing. Nevertheless, the publishers cannot be held responsible for any errors or omissions or for changes in the details given in this book or for the consequences of any reliance on the information it provides. This does not affect your statutory rights. We have tried to ensure accuracy in this book, but things do change and we would be grateful if readers would advise us of any inaccuracies they may encounter.

We have taken all reasonable steps to ensure that the walks and cycle rides in this book are safe and achievable by people with a realistic level of fitness. However, all outdoor activities involve a degree of risk and the publishers accept no responsibility for any injuries caused to readers while following these walks and cycle rides. For more advice on walking and cycling in safety see pages 16–17.

Some of the walks and cycle routes may appear in other AA books.

Visit AA Publishing at theAA.com/shop

Printed and bound in China by C&C

A04393

CONTENTS

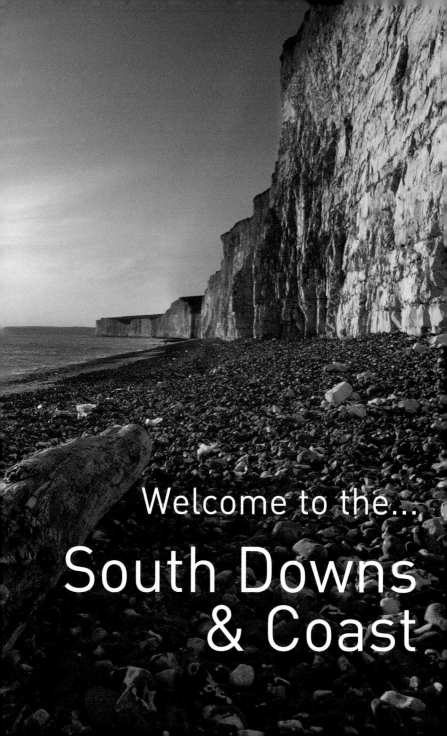

Welcome to the...

South Downs & Coast

You get a marvellously exhilarating feeling of being on top of the world by venturing up the South Downs, a chalky range of hills that stretches from the historic city of Winchester to the dizzying heights of Beachy Head. Whether you are walking, horse-riding, mountain biking, paragliding or simply admiring the peace and open space, the white chalk tracks of the South Downs Way feel hundreds of miles from London, with only skylarks for company. On the inland side of the ridge are steep slopes of turf and vast views across the patchwork of woods and fields of the area known as the Weald. On the other side, long dry valleys stretch towards glimpses of the sea. This landscape has a strong sense of the past: many prehistoric mounds and field boundaries are still visible.

Though not particularly high, the Downs have a great presence both from the sea and from the land where they rise like a green wave. They look bare and dry in the east, and more wooded in the west. It's a view people have cherished for thousands of years – Romano-British villas like Bignor and later stately homes were positioned in some of the best spots for to view them. Now these hills are preserved in their entirety as Britain's newest

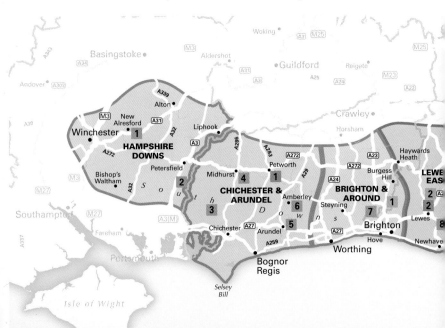

national park, the South Downs National Park, which extends between Winchester and Eastbourne, and includes much of northwest Sussex too.

The coast is where seaside holidays were practically invented. Brighton developed as a fashionable resort, followed by places like Eastbourne and Bexhill. Railways brought the visitors in, and they took excursions to rural beauty spots, village inns and tea gardens – many of which are still thriving today. Writers and garden designers have also treasured this countryside and left their legacy of evocative places to visit.

More than any other seaside area in Britain, the best-loved towns are packed with history and architectural beauty and have an individual and civilised feel. Partly it's the influence of London – it's still easy to get down by train, and the area has long been a retreat for cultural and arty élites. You can get a feel for places as different as vibrant Brighton, quirky Hastings Old Town and Lewes, or cultural Winchester, Chichester, Arundel and Rye from their myriad events and festivals. There's a variety of ways to enjoy the South Downs and Sussex coast, but you must pick your way carefully. This guide selects the cream and we hope it inspires you to return again and again.

6 Walk start point

1 Cycle start point

2 Tour start point

1

2

3

ESSENTIAL SIGHTS

Stride out on the chalky paths of the South Downs Way, or take your bike, ride a horse or paraglide... sample the highly thought-of local wines, the South Downs lamb and Hampshire watercress or go alfresco as you barbecue fresh fish on the beach... experience the hush of the reed-fringed waterways and rich bird life of the water meadows and wetlands... follow the literary trail of Jane Austen, Winnie-the-Pooh, Rudyard Kipling or Virginia Woolf and the Bloomsbury Set... see behind the scenes at some of Britain's stateliest homes... time your visit to catch the big occasion of your choice, from the Goodwood Festival of Speed to massive art events in Chichester, Brighton and Arundel... enjoy the best family-friendly animal attractions such as Marwell Wildlife, Drusillas and Brighton Sea Life Centre.

1 Birling Gap
The pebble beach at Birling Gap, accessed by a stout flight of steps, is set below the dramatic white chalk cliffs of the Seven Sisters. Both the beach and the cliff tops are popular with walkers.

2 Eastbourne
The magnificent Carpet Gardens, set between the bandstand and the pier, are the dazzling centrepiece of Eastbourne's promenade in spring and summer.

3 Ditchling Beacon
There are many off-road downland cycling routes near the historic village of Ditchling in East Sussex.

4 Brighton
The spectacular Royal Pavilion lends an exotic air to this area of the big and bustling town of Brighton. It was remodelled by John Nash between 1815 and 1822 for the Prince Regent.

4

6 Camber Sands

The wonderful soft golden beach, backed by ridges of sand dunes, makes Camber Sands an ideal location for an old-fashioned English bucket-and-spade seaside holiday.

6

7 South Downs Way

Characterised by dry valleys, rolling grassland, and views over the Weald to the north and the sea to the south, the South Downs Way follows old routes and droveways. The trail is shared by walkers, cyclists, and horse-riders.

8 Beachy Head

A lone lighthouse, built of Cornish granite in 1902, stands guard at the foot of the dramatic white cliffs at Beachy Head.

9 Devil's Dyke

There are great views of farmland, downland and the sea from this famous beauty spot on the South Downs Way. The Dyke is best explored on the circular Access Trail.

10 Chichester

The graceful spire of Chichester Cathedral was rebuilt in the 19th century by Sir Gilbert Scott. The cathedral is known for its modern art; works to be seen here are a window by Marc Chagall, a tapestry by John Piper and a painting by Graham Sutherland.

7

Day One

The South Downs has long been a popular weekend destination, easily reached by car or train from London. You can stay in a seaside hotel, a country pub or sophisticated town house. This itinerary, based on Lewes, gives a taster of the variety the area has to offer.

Friday night

Arrive in Lewes by train or car. A good place to stay is the Pelham House hotel (St Andrew's Lane. Tel: 01273 488600; www.pelhamhouse.com), an imposing building dating from the 1600s, with the atmosphere of a stylish country house yet right in the town centre. Stay and eat in their brasserie with its inventive international cuisine or, if you have a car, drive out for a meal in the smart but quite informal restaurant at the Jolly Sportsman in the tiny village of East Chiltington. They also serve bar meals here. You can sample the local Harveys ale in one of the inviting Lewes town centre pubs, such as the John Harvey.

Saturday morning

After breakfast explore the fascinating corners of the Lewes twittens (narrow lanes) on foot, browse the secondhand bookshops and antiques markets, visit the castle and head down Keere Street to the Grange Gardens. If you're here on the first Saturday in the month you will catch the local Farmers' Market. If the weather's fine, walk up on to the South Downs and take in the views from Mount Caburn, where you'll often see graceful paragliders overhead. Or head down to shingly Seaford by train or car, and stroll up Seaford Head to see the staggeringly beautiful view of the Seven Sisters.

Saturday lunch

At the heart of the lower town in Cliffe, Bill's is much more than a greengrocer. Choose your lunch from tempting fare such as salads, quiches and smoothies, freshly made from their own produce.

Saturday afternoon

Today's trains from Lewes give a smooth and scenic ride to either Rye or Hastings in around an hour, skirting both the South Downs escarpment and the coast around Pevensey Castle. Take time to explore the cobbled streets and classy shops in Rye and perhaps hire a bike and follow the Sustrans cycle path to the glorious beach at Camber Sands. Or you could stroll through Hastings Old Town and climb up the steep steps or use the cliff railway for a bracing ramble along the cliff tops in the Hastings Country Park on East Hill – there's also plenty to keep the children occupied on the sea front, such as a miniature golf course.

Saturday night

An excellent choice for dinner would be Rye's picturesque 15th-century Mermaid Inn (where you could spend the night) or you could stop off at one of the cheerful café-restaurants in Hastings Old Town such as Pomegranate, Latham's or Harris's in George Street or the High Street. Head back to Lewes after supper.

Day Two

Our second and final day in the South Downs takes in England's top seaside resort – cosmopolitan Brighton. The city is a rich mix of Regency architectural heritage, specialist shops, beachfront sports, gay pubs and clubs, vibrant nightlife, lively arts and year-round events. The undoubted highlight of the day is a visit to the Royal Pavilion, with its lavish Chinese-style interiors, magnificent furniture and restored Regency gardens.

Sunday morning

Fifteen minutes on the train in the other direction from Lewes will take you to lively Brighton. Browse the stalls in the Sunday morning antiques market by the station, and wander through the funky North Laine, where wonderful individual shops offer everything from the latest designer fashions and retro 50s clothes to unique jewellery, oriental furniture and musical instruments. Stop off at one of the many cafés and bars for a mid-morning espresso and to enjoy a spot of people-watching.

Sunday lunch

Pop into Terre à Terre, a chic vegetarian restaurant situated near the Pavilion, or try one of many other excellent eateries, including trendy cafés and traditional pubs, to be found in the Lanes.

Sunday afternoon

Visit Brighton Pavilion, one of the most extraordinary palaces in Europe, which was developed by the extravagant Prince Regent in the early 19th century. The building conjures up an Indian fantasy from outside: inside it has a dazzling variety of Chinese-inspired décor, with a great sense of fun, and there's a great tea room upstairs. If you have the time, cross the re-created Regency gardens and have a look at the eclectic displays in the free Brighton Museum and Art Gallery. Highlights include the costume, pottery and furniture collections, tribal arts and lots on the quirky and seamy sides of Brighton, past and present. The café here is good too: it's on a balcony above the main gallery.

After seeing the Pavilion you can stroll along the seafront, take a white-knuckle ride on the pier, explore the tiny fishing museum, have a drink at a beach bar, ride the Volks Railway to the Marina, or even hire a surfboard if the conditions are right. Or just relax on the beach and watch the world go by. If you like visiting aquariums, the Brighton Sea Life Centre is one of the best of its kind, with many original Victorian fittings.

Lingering on into the evening, catch some jazz or cabaret at the Joogleberry Playhouse, see alternative comedy at Komedia, or watch a film at the Duke of York's, one of the region's top arts cinemas. For eating you're spoiled for choice: there's a huge variety of places in The Lanes, just inland from the pier.

Route facts

MINIMUM TIME The time stated for completing each route is the estimated minimum time that a reasonably fit family group of walkers or cyclists would take to complete the circuit. This does not allow for rest or refreshment stops.

OS MAP Each route is shown on a map. However, some detail is lost because of the restrictions imposed by scale, so for this reason we recommend that you use the maps in conjunction with a more detailed Ordnance Survey map. The relevant map for each walk or cycle ride is listed.

START This indicates the start location and parking area. This is a six-figure grid reference prefixed by two letters showing which 62.5-mile (100km) square of the National Grid it refers to. You'll find more information on grid references on most Ordnance Survey maps.

CYCLE HIRE We list, within reason, the nearest cycle hire shop/centre.

❶ Here we highlight any potential difficulties or dangers along the cycle ride or walk. If a particular route is suitable for older, fitter children we say so here. Also, we give guidelines of a route's suitability for younger children, for example the symbol 8+ indicates that the route can probably be attempted by children aged 8 years and above.

Walks & Cycle Rides

Each walk and cycle ride has a panel giving information for the walker and cyclist, including the distance, terrain, nature of the paths, and where to park your car.

WALKING

All of the walks are suitable for families, but less experienced family groups, especially those with younger children, should try the shorter walks. Route finding is usually straightforward, but the maps are for guidance only and we recommend that you always take the relevant Ordnance Survey map with you.

Risks

Although each walk has been researched with a view to minimising any risks, no walk in the countryside can be considered to be completely free from risk. Walking in the outdoors will always require a degree of common sense and judgement to ensure that it is as safe as possible, especially for young children.

• Be particularly careful on cliff paths and in upland terrain, where the consequences of a slip can be serious.

• Remember to check tidal conditions before walking on the seashore.

• Some sections of route are by, or cross, busy roads.

Remember traffic is a danger even on minor country lanes.

• Be careful around farmyard machinery and livestock.

• Be prepared for the consequences of changes in the weather and check the forecast before you set out.

• Ensure the whole family is properly equipped, wearing suitable clothing and a good pair of boots or sturdy walking shoes. Take waterproof clothing with you and a torch if you are walking in the winter months.

• Remember the weather can change quickly at any time of the year, and in moorland and heathland areas, mist and fog can make route-finding much harder. In summer, take account of the heat and sun by wearing a hat, sunscreen and carrying enough water.

• On walks away from centres of population you should carry a mobile phone, whistle and, if possible, a survival bag. If you do have an accident requiring emergency services, make a note of your position as accurately as possible and dial 999 (112 on a mobile).

CYCLING

In devising the cycle rides in this guide, every effort has been made to use designated cycle paths, or to link them with quiet country lanes and waymarked byways and bridleways. In a few cases, some fairly busy B-roads have been used to join up with quieter routes.

Rules of the road

• Ride in single file on narrow and busy roads.

• Be alert, look and listen for traffic, especially on narrow lanes and blind bends and be extra careful when descending steep hills, as loose gravel or a poor road surface can lead to an accident.

• In wet weather make sure that you keep an appropriate distance between you and other riders.

• Make sure you indicate your intentions clearly.

• Brush up on *The Highway Code* before venturing out on to the road.

Off-road safety code of conduct

• Only ride where you know it is legal to do so. Cyclists are not allowed to cycle on public footpaths (yellow waymarks). The only 'rights of way' open to cyclists are bridleways (blue markers) and unsurfaced tracks, known as byways, which are open to all traffic and waymarked in red.

• Canal tow paths: you need a permit to cycle on some stretches of tow path (www. waterscape.com). Remember that access paths can be steep and slippery so always push your bike under low bridges and by locks.

• Always yield to walkers and horses, giving adequate warning of your approach.

• Don't expect to cycle at high speeds.

• Keep to the main trail to avoid any unnecessary erosion to the area beside the trail and to prevent skidding, especially in wet weather conditions.

• Remember to follow the Country Code.

Preparing your bicycle

Check the wheels, tyres, brakes and cables. Lubricate hubs, pedals, gear mechanisms and cables. Make sure you have a pump, a bell, a rear rack to carry panniers and a set of lights.

Equipment

• A cycling helmet provides essential protection.

• Make sure you are visible to other road users, by wearing light-coloured or luminous clothing in daylight and sashes or reflective strips in failing light and darkness.

• Take extra clothes with you, depending on the season, and a wind/waterproof jacket.

• Carry a basic tool kit, a pump, a strong lock and a first aid kit.

• Always carry enough water for your outing.

Walk Map Legend

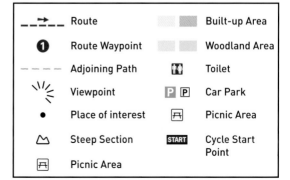

➔ Route			Built-up Area
❶ Route Waypoint			Woodland Area
– – – – Adjoining Path		🚻	Toilet
Viewpoint		P P	Car Park
• Place of interest		🪑	Picnic Area
⌂ Steep Section		START	Cycle Start Point
🪑 Picnic Area			

QUEEN ELIZABETH COUNTRY PARK

Hampshire Downs

The South Downs Way begins its journey from the ancient capital of Winchester, where the water meadows almost reach the cathedral precincts. Not far away, the steam trains of the Watercress Line puff through the rolling landscape. The steep beech 'hangers' around Selborne and the clear trout streams of the Meon and Arle valleys haven't changed much since the times of Jane Austen, Izaak Walton (of *Compleat Angler* fame) and the naturalist Gilbert White.

1 Walk start point

BUTSER HILL

Unmissable attractions

Take in the aerial view of Winchester from the cathedral tower...wander through Winchester's water meadows to the spectacularly unchanged medieval almshouse that is St Cross Hospital...get face to face with the giraffes at Marwell Wildlife ...tuck in to fresh watercress scones at New Alresford and take a ride on the Watercress Line...spend an afternoon watching cricket at historic Broadhalfpenny Down, where the first recorded match took place...evoke the Iron Age at the hill-fort on Old Winchester Hill, a prized nature reserve for downland wildflowers...follow the steps of literary pilgrims to Jane Austen's house and see where she wrote some of her most celebrated novels...see where the pioneering naturalist Gilbert White lived and the wooded slopes where he made his observations at Selborne.

1 East Meon

The River Meon flows lazily past the picturesque thatched cottages in East Meon, one of Hampshire's loveliest villages.

2 Queen Elizabeth Country Park

Hampshire's biggest country park gives access to woodland and downland with miles of trails suitable for cyclists, walkers and horse-riders alike.

3 Selborne

The quiet village of Selborne was the home of the famous naturalist Gilbert White, author of *The Natural History and Antiquities of Selborne*.

4 Winchester

The cathedral, which is set among green lawns and mature trees in tranquil Cathedral Close, is perhaps Winchester's greatest glory.

5 Alresford

A pleasant riverside walk in delightful Alresford passes the thatched former fulling mill which dates from the 13th century.

BISHOP'S WALTHAM
MAP REF SU5617

The place name of this quiet little shopping town gives a clue to its past, as it is the location of one of the bishop's palaces of the diocese of Winchester, the richest diocese in England. Now in graceful ruins and roofless (maintained by English Heritage), the palace was clearly a fairly opulent place to stay for travelling bishops. The dry-moated site is a few steps away from the high street (it is signposted down a small turning opposite the Crown pub) and was mostly built during the 14th and 15th centuries by bishops Wykeham (the founder of Winchester College) and Beaufort. As you enter the palace, you pass between the guesthouse lodgings on the right and the bakehouse and brewhouse to the left. Across the lawn, the west tower, Great Hall (with some tracery still visible in its windows, and one apex at its original height) and the kitchen hint at the building's former glories.

CHAWTON MAP REF SU7137

Jane Austen's house at Chawton has become an international literary shrine, helped by popular TV and feature film adaptations of her novels. Once on a busy road junction between Guildford, Winchester and Portsmouth, the unspoiled village of Chawton today is quieter than it was in Jane Austen's time, but you can easily imagine her walking out to visit neighbours.

Jane's brother Edward installed his widowed mother and sisters Jane and Cassandra at Chawton in 1809; his improvements for the house included the sash window with its Gothic arches on the right of the entrance. Cassandra kept house and her mother looked after the garden. This left Jane, whose main duty was preparing breakfast, free to write at her tiny 12-sided table, alerted to visitors by a creaking door that was deliberately left un-oiled. It was here that Jane revised *Sense and Sensibility* and *Pride and Prejudice*, published in 1811 and 1813, and wrote *Mansfield Park, Emma* and *Persuasion*.

The rooms and gardens are as they would have been in Regency times, with a 'square piano', which visitors are very welcome to play, and numerous family mementoes: the family tea pot, the patchwork quilt made by the three ladies with tiny lozenge-shaped patches, family letters and portraits, and the donkey carriage that took them shopping in the nearby market town of Alton. Perhaps most evocative for devotees of the novels are Jane and Cassandra's topaz crosses, presents from their sailor brother Charles – Fanny Price, heroine of *Mansfield Park*, also receives an amber cross from her sea-faring brother, and suffers much social embarrassment about the choice of gold chains to wear with it.

■ Insight

BAKER'S WINE MERCHANTS
At 6 High Street in Bishop's Waltham, Baker's Wine Merchants was founded in 1617 and originally served the palace; its original cellars are now a separate wine bar. Today the shop sells its own wines from the nearby Titchfield vineyard, around which it offers occasional tours during the summer months.

HINTON AMPNER

MAP REF SU5927

Sheep stray obliviously across the drive that curves up through the park towards Hinton Ampner house. The setting of house, gardens and park form a perfect composition: from a distance the house, on a notable rise, is prominent, but the gardens lie hidden in a belt of green, and have a secretive quality that only reveals itself when you are close.

The estate was left to the National Trust by Ralph Dutton in 1985: Dutton was much influenced by great gardens such as Sissinghurst and Hidcote, which inspired him to create those at Hinton Ampner as a series of 'rooms' divided by low hedges, leading from one mood to another. In front of the house stretches a long lawn, looking out over the Downs, then you drop into another part, past a temple and walk up a sloping crescent between the philadelphus that blossoms in early summer. The walled garden is subject to a long-term restoration programme – if you want the details, chat to one of the gardeners. At the edge of the gardens, the transition into rolling, old-fashioned parkland appears seamless, but close up you find that the gardens are bounded by a hidden ditch, or 'ha-ha', with strategic cattle grids giving access for strolls in the park.

Dutton wasn't keen on the Victorian style, and remodelled what was mainly a Victorian Gothic pile into a neo-Georgian mansion in 1935. He had to do it all over again 25 years later after a disastrous fire, but most of his superb collection of Georgian and Regency furniture, and Italian artworks, survived – together they

■ Visit

JANE AUSTEN'S TOMB

A mystifying illness took Jane Austen to Winchester in search of medical attention in 1817. She died there that year aged 41 and is commemorated by a grave slab in the north aisle of Winchester Cathedral. The marker makes no mention of her writing – she was published anonymously in her lifetime – but waxes lyrical about her personal qualities: '... The benevolence of her heart, the sweetness of her composure, the extraordinary endowments of her mind, obtained the regard of all who knew her, and the warmest love of her intimate connections...'

■ Visit

THE TIN CHURCH IN THE WOODS

At Bramdean Common, not far from Hinton Ampner, is the so-called Church in the Woods, a corrugated iron church erected in just five days in 1883 by a Romany gypsy community. It's no grand work of architecture, but worth seeing for its touching simplicity. There's still a local Romany community, and the graves in the tiny churchyard are neatly kept.

represent the personal tastes of a great collector. The classical interior, which includes a ceiling by Robert Adam, has a bright, pristine look, but the restoration is very carefully done. In the North Drawing Room photo albums chronicle the house's story, including the fire, the rebuilding, its wartime days as a school, and the garden. From the windows there are captivating views over the parkland and surroundings. There's a café in the old stable block, and an own-brew pub, the Flower Pots, at nearby Cheriton.

MARWELL WILDLIFE
MAP REF SU5022

Far removed from the idea of animals miserably stuck in cages, Marwell – a registered charity – was in 1972 one of the first zoos in the country to be set up for the purpose of endangered species conservation. It is set in rolling parkland around a country house, Marwell Hall, and has a worldwide selection including lemurs, tropical creepy-crawlies, zebras, antelopes, tigers, snow leopards, white rhinos and meerkats. The animals roam about in generously sized enclosures and, because of the lie of the land and thanks to various raised platforms and other devices, visitors can observe the beasts from various angles and heights. You can get face to face with giraffes in their paddock, peer through a window and see penguins swimming underwater in Penguin World, spy on the movements of the many big cats or meet the more familiar farmyard animals in Encounter Village. Watch out for the posted times of the daily keeper talks; if you're feeling intrepid (and rich) you can splash out on an Animal Encounter, where you go behind the scenes and feed an animal and meet its keeper.

With 2.5 miles (4km) of paths, there's a lot to see here, and you need a full day to take it all in – if you've enjoyed your visit the annual season tickets are good value. It's worth coming at any time of year, though bear in mind that during the heat of the day animals are dozier, and there are after-hours 'sunset safaris' when the animals are often livelier and you get the place to yourself. There is a miniature train ride (extra charge) and a land train will transport you around the site and save your feet. Public transport to the zoo is limited, but there are buses from Eastleigh and Winchester stations on Sundays.

MEON VALLEY MAP REF SU6117

Izaak Walton, known as the father of angling, loved to fish in the clear waters of the River Meon, still regarded today as one of Britain's best trout rivers. He famously penned his appreciation of the pastoral pastime in *The Compleat Angler*, published in 1653. Travelling between the string of attractive villages, from Wickham in the south to East Meon, you'll see the signs for trout fisheries where you can try your hand at the sport and get the idea of what it was that enthused Walton so much.

With some notable exceptions, the scenery here is pleasantly mild rather than dramatic. The valley's disused railway line, running from West Meon to Wickham, is now the particularly attractive Meon Valley Trail, a level route

■ Insight

RETURN TO THE WILD

Many endangered species have been bred at Marwell for eventual release into the wild. These include golden lion tamarins who roam free in the park, and the famous Przewalski's horse, the world's only remaining truly wild horse, which has now been re-introduced in Hungary, Mongolia and Eelmoor Marsh, near Farnborough in Kent. Natterjack toads raised at Marwell are eventually taken to Cumbria and sand lizards are bred for release in the New Forest. Animals that are kept for display and not for release are reared in the UK and not taken from the wild.

■ Insight

BROADHALFPENNY DOWN

At a crossroads on the top of the Downs between Hambledon and East Meon, stands the Bat and Ball pub. This historic premises once functioned as a pavilion for Broadhalfpenny Down cricket ground, across the road, and is regarded as the cradle of cricket. The first recorded cricket match took place here around 1750, when it was the home ground of the formidable Hambledon Cricket Club. Indeed, the murky origins of cricket go back to shepherds playing on the South Downs, with balls of compact wool and gates as wickets. From the 1790s the ground was disused until Winchester College acquired it in the early 20th century. Since the 1950s the Broadhalfpenny Brigands have played here and it makes for a most bucolic place for watching a game on a summer's day, with a rustic wooden pavilion and a line of trees on the other.

for walkers, horse-riders and cyclists. You can enjoy pottering around on a bike along the narrow lanes that connect the villages on the east side of the valley (rather than use the busy A32), and if you want more testing walking you can tackle part of the South Downs Way, which crosses the Meon Valley at Exton and climbs to the viewpoints on Beacon Hill and Old Winchester Hill.

Further south, the Forest of Bere, a 865-acre (350ha) fragment of an ancient royal hunting forest, has numerous fine waymarked trails and picnic areas; there are also three designated car parks (West Walk, Woodend and Upperford Copse), and an exciting mountain bike trail that begins from West Walk.

One of Hampshire's most photogenic villages and endowed with two pubs (one is the Izaak Walton, where you can raise a glass to the great angler), East Meon has the infant river running along the middle of its quaint main street, lined with attractive brick and half-timbered houses, some thatched, and there's still a village smithy here – in operation for more than a century. On a rise somewhat apart from the rest of the village, the Church of All Saints dates from the mid-12th century and has rounded Norman arches at the crossing of the chancel and the nave, and a wonderful Tournai font (one of four in Hampshire; another is at Winchester Cathedral), with carvings depicting Adam and Eve and an assembly of beasts. Also look for a tombstone inside inscribed 'Amens Plenty' thought to cover the graves of four Parliamentary soldiers who were killed during the Civil War. Just across the road you can glimpse the medieval Court House, where the powerful Bishops of Winchester once held court. Today the building is occasionally used for theatrical performances.

Old Winchester Hill National Nature Reserve is a marvellously dramatic stretch of chalk downland, where the steep slope has managed to escape modern farming, enabling a great range of wildlife to flourish. There are badgers, roe deer and dormice in the woodland, while more than 30 species of butterfly (including silver spotted skippers and speckled wood) can be found, and chalk-loving wildflowers such as orchids grow in profusion on the grasslands. From the main car park, an easy level track leads towards the fascinating Iron Age hill fort of Winchester Hill, within the ramparts of which are Bronze Age burial mounds, or barrows, which have never been excavated. There's also a very pleasant waymarked circular walk (it takes up to 2 hours) that leads walkers downhill and along the hillside through woodland. For some more detailed information, pick up a leaflet at the car park and consult the interpretative boards. The nature reserve is signposted from the A32 at Warnford; the road gets more scenic as you travel towards the Royal Navy communications school at HMS *Mercury*, with wide views.

MID-HANTS RAILWAY (WATERCRESS LINE)
MAP REF SU5832

Known generally as the Watercress Line because it was once used to transport Hampshire watercress to Covent Garden Market in London, this line provides a fabulous nostalgia-fest as well as being an unforgettable way of reaching New Alresford from Alton. Alton itself, with its long Georgian High Street and bustling Tuesday market, is served by direct main-line trains from London Waterloo, so you can easily make a full day of it and maybe return home with your own cargo of watercress. All tickets give unlimited travel for a day and there are spaces for wheelchairs. The Old Goods Shed shop at Alresford has plenty of souvenirs to browse.

Four years after the line closed in 1973, an army of enthusiasts reopened it, and it's clearly been a labour of love. Volunteers are dressed in period rail-staff uniform, and the station buildings are immaculately tended, with antique advertising signs proclaiming the virtues of products called Nosegay and Rinso, and well-travelled old leather luggage trunks on the platform. Trains are pulled by steam and diesel locos, and most of the carriages are the familiar post-1951 variety, although one dates from 1947. At Ropley station, the engineering centre of the line, you can view the loco yard, and you might spot The Shant, a building that housed the 'navvies' who built the line in the 1860s. Check out the website for details of the regular *Thomas the Tank Engine* Days, when Thomas races alongside his engine friends, October Wizard Week, when fancy dress is very much encouraged, gourmet dining trips and the popular Real Ale Train, which serves passengers ale from breweries in Hampshire and the nearby counties. If you really want to splash out, spend a day learning to drive a locomotive.

■ Insight

WATERCRESS

There's been a revival in watercress on the dinner table in recent years, and as well as a delicious salad vegetable, it's also an ingredient in a variety of products, including pesto, scones and pâté. The Arle valley is the biggest watercress-producing area in Britain, with the growing season running from September to June. Six crops grow each year, taking six weeks from seeding to plucking. The beds are large rectangular concrete trays that are fed by mineral-rich springs, and the picking is done by hand, by pickers in wellies or waders. Alresford's Watercress Festival on the third Sunday in May brings in big crowds for cookery demonstrations, children's events and live music.

A Walk Around the Alresfords

New Alresford (pronounced Allsford) is not very new at all. It was 'new' in 1200 when the Bishop of Winchester decided to expand the original Alresford. Two fires in the 17th century destroyed most of the original timber-framed houses. The rebuilding resulted in the Georgian architecture you see today. Close to both New and Old Alresford you will find an intricate network of clear chalk streams, rivulets and channels that form the rivers Arle and Itchen and the Candover Stream. Since Victorian times these streams and rivers have played a vital role in the production of watercress, which today is celebrated in an annual Watercress Festival.

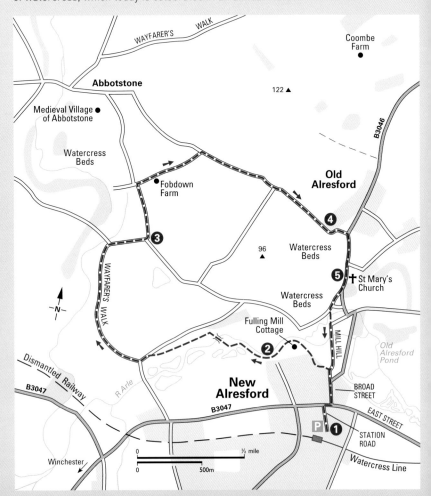

Route Directions

1 From the car park walk down Station Road to the T-junction with West Street. Turn right, then left down Broad Street and keep left at the bottom along Mill Hill. Half way down turn left into Ladywell Lane and soon you will join the river bank and pass the attractive, timbered and thatched Fulling Mill Cottage which straddles the River Arle.

2 Continue to the bottom of Dean Lane and keep to the riverside path. Cross a footbridge over the river, and ascend to pass some cottages. Shortly, a lane merges from your right; follow it for 50yds (46m), then fork right onto the Wayfarer's Walk and continue to a junction of tracks. Bear right uphill to a lane.

3 Turn left, descend to Fobdown Farm and take the track on the right beside the farm buildings. On reaching a T-junction of tracks, turn right and follow the established track for just over 0.5 mile (800m), gently descending into Old Alresford.

4 Pass watercress beds on your right and follow the now metalled lane left, past houses. Turn right beside the green to reach the B3046. Cross over and follow the pavement right to a lane opposite St Mary's Church.

5 Having visited the church, cross the road and turn left along the pavement to a grass triangle by a junction. Bear right along the lane and take the footpath ahead over a stream and beside watercress beds back to Mill Hill and Broad Street.

Route facts

DISTANCE/TIME 4 miles (6.4km) 2h

MAP OS Explorer 132 Winchester

START Pay-and-display car park off Station Road, New Alresford; grid ref SU 588325

TRACKS Riverside paths, tracks, field, woodland paths and roads

GETTING TO THE START New Alresford is signposted off the A31 between Winchester and Alton, 6 miles (9.7km) east of Winchester. On the main village street, follow signs to the Watercress Line to locate the parking area.

THE PUB The Bell Hotel, New Alresford, Tel: 01962 732429

❶ New Alresford can be busy with cars; riverside paths are near water in places; take care crossing the B3046.

NEW ALRESFORD

MAP REF SU5832

Regarded as Hampshire's finest Georgian town and at the southern terminus of the Mid-Hants Railway, New Alresford has an eye-catching mixture of colour-washed and brick houses along its long, sloping street. It is a rather chic shopping venue, with a great variety of classy, individual shops, as well as a good range of tea rooms. There's a lively Thursday market in tree-lined Broad Street, with a producers' market every third Thursday of the month, offering an array of jams, watercress, chocolates and other local goodies. In West Street, Mange2 Deli has a fantastic range of cheeses, and local chocolates made in nearby Preston Candover.

The town was rebuilt after two huge fires in 1689 and 1736, and its Georgian uniformity is the key to its charm. The character has been safeguarded by a Board of Trustees, which has attended to part of the town centre since 1887. Beyond Broad Street, you can follow Mill Hill down into Ladywell Lane and reach a stretch of the River Arle by a former fulling mill that straddles the river. The path leads along a delightful stretch of river, populated by trout and otters, and passes close to some of the valley's many watercress beds.

QUEEN ELIZABETH COUNTRY PARK MAP REF SU7218

Butser Hill, now bisected by the A3 south of Petersfield, is the highest point on the South Downs. The Country Park gives open access to 1,400 acres (560ha) of woodland and downland within the East Hampshire Area of Outstanding Natural Beauty, with 20 miles (32km) of trails for walkers, cyclists and horse-riders, a demonstration Iron Age farm, an adventure playground and a varied programme of events.

Most of Butser Hill is designated a Site of Special Scientific Interest and since 1998 as a National Nature Reserve. It's one of the largest areas of chalky grassland in Hampshire, with yew, beech and conifers providing additional habitats to a rich population of wild flowers, butterflies and lichens.

SELBORNE MAP REF SU7433

Gilbert White's House takes up a long section of Selborne's characterful High Street, as befits the home of its most celebrated resident. White (1720–93) is best known for his *Natural History and Antiquities of Selborne*, observations of the natural world recorded in the form of a series of letters, which has never been out of print since 1789. Both readable and ground-breaking, White's works inspired both the scientific observations of Darwin and the more poetic traditions of English nature writing. He was the first to describe the importance of earthworms in what we would now call the ecosystem, and helped to prove the phenomenon of bird migrations – previously people had speculated that birds hibernated in holes in the ground.

As was still possible in the 18th century, White managed to be in the forefront of knowledge in more than one field. He was an antiquarian, an active clergyman and an innovative gardener, doing the best he could on a modest income to follow the horticultural and landscaping advances of his day. His garden, now restored, is a delight, with walks meandering round the different areas, right up to the woods. The house re-creates the rooms as they would have been in the 18th century: White's study has a dissected bird, grasses, a mouse nest and a deer skull alongside leather-bound volumes, drafts of sermons and a seed catalogue. Downstairs, you can see the original manuscript of the *Natural History*. Also on site, the Oates Museum commemorates Captain Lawrence Oates of Captain Scott's ill-fated Antarctic Expedition, and his uncle Frank Oates, a naturalist who died young in Africa. Their descendant Robert Washington Oates helped with the purchase of the Gilbert White House in 1954.

Selborne offers some easy walks into the complicated countryside of woods and valleys that White observed so closely, such as the stroll through the churchyard to the enticing grassy valleys of Short Lythe and Long Lythe (National Trust), surrounded by beech woods.

The sad remains of the Selborne Yew, thought to be around 1,400 years old, stand covered by honeysuckle in the churchyard. Felled by a gale in 1990, this much-loved landmark was replanted but sadly failed to survive. A highly polished section from its largest branch is on display in the church porch, with dates going back to 1509 marked on the tree rings. The church door with its scrolly ironwork is even older, dating from the 13th century. Inside, the church is wide and plain, dating from about 1180. The sombre black slab in front of the altar

■ Activity

WALK TO WHITE'S ZIG-ZAG PATH

Walk from the village car park (behind the Selborne Arms) past White's house and down Gracious Street with its thatched cottages. Where the lane bends right, go left through a gate, follow the path over a stile then turn left along the bottom of the woods where there are views across White's garden to the village. At a National Trust sign take White's Zig-Zag path (cut by him and his brother in 1753) up to Selborne Common with views across to the Surrey Heaths; return down the Zig-Zag path and go straight on through a kissing gate back to the car park.

■ Activity

WAYFARER'S WALK

This waymarked long-distance path (look for the WW markers), running 71 miles (114km) from Emsworth in Hampshire to Inkpen Beacon in Berkshire, is a good route out into some lovely chalkland countryside. On the way it passes through Hambledon and Droxford in the Meon Valley, Hinton Ampner estate (look for the signpost by the gate over the road near the estate church), Cheriton (where you can walk around a Civil War battlefield), New Alresford and over Watership Down.

commemorates the life of Gilbert White's grandfather; White himself is buried in the northeast corner of the churchyard, where his simple headstone is almost sunk into the ground.

Selborne has a pottery; the Hampshire Artists Cooperative share the same gallery, and a gallery showing the work of mouth and foot artists who have attained high artistic standards.

WINCHESTER MAP REF SU4730

Home to the world's longest medieval cathedral and one of Britain's great public (fee-paying) schools, and with a story that stretches back from Roman times, Winchester provides a heady walk through two millennia of history, along its main street, through alleys and gardens, past charitable almshouses and around the Cathedral Close. The city's sheer physical beauty and prized position by water meadows, has a well-heeled air that permeates the speciality and high street shops, classy eating places and Britain's largest farmers' market. The Square and Parchment Street are best for independent shops and there are more in Little and Great Minster Streets, St Thomas Street and Southgate Street, all near the cathedral.

There's a good park-and-ride at junction 10 of the M3, and the Bikeabout scheme gives unlimited use of a bike in the city for a year for £20 (includes free map and helmet), which you pick up from the tourist information centre or from Winchester Shopmobility (in Brooks Shopping Centre). Summer festivals get the city into full swing, particularly the Hat Fair in July, when some often outrageously forward street theatre takes place, and audience participation can hardly be avoided. Winchester also has a strong army presence – the Royal Hampshire Regiment, Royal Green Jackets and Royal Hussars are based here, and there are six regimental museums at Peninsula Barracks.

The city centre is laid out on a simple grid that dates from the 880s when King Alfred the Great, the first king to unite England, set up his capital here, though the main axis along the High Street goes back to Roman times. Getting your bearings here is easy. From the top end of the High Street, you wander through the 13th-century West Gate, one of the city's surviving ancient gateways, past the bow-fronted former premises of the *Hampshire Chronicle* and half-timbered God Begot House, and the ornate stone Market Cross, with its massive figurine of Alfred. Further on, a substantially chunkier, sword-wielding statue of Alfred stands in The Broadway outside the Gothic, high Victorian town hall. At the River Itchen you can take a tour round the City Mill, a beautifully preserved National Trust-owned watermill, or continue up to the top of St Giles' Hill, a rural oasis, for views over the city. There is also a very alluring riverside path along The Weirs, a gorgeous area of city park that peeps across the Itchen into back gardens.

The City Museum presents highlights from the city's past, with an array of reconstructed city shops – a chemists, tobacconists, and Bosley's – the latter a tiny shop in a front room. Upstairs, models show the development of the city, recognisable in layout from the early years, and there are archaeological finds as well as coins that were hammered at Winchester's own mint, which existed from the reign of Alfred to Henry III.

Winchester Cathedral and its graceful close fill up a sizeable area of the historic core. There's been a place of worship here since the 7th century, and it is the start of the Pilgrims' Way, which ends at Canterbury Cathedral. Nowadays it attracts Dan Brown fans on the trail of *The Da Vinci Code*. In the film the north transept doubled as The Vatican. The present building dates from William I's scheme to build the largest cathedral in the world, mostly using stone from the Isle of Wight, though what you first see is the nave with its pointed arcades in the graceful Perpendicular style of the 15th century. But at the crossing the arches suddenly become rounded Norman, and as you walk further into the chancel you get an idea how much it has subsided, as its sloping floor and arches are well out of true. Seek out the memorial to Jane Austen in the north aisle and the tomb of Izaak Walton (author of *The Compleat Angler*; he is buried in the south transept), the statue of William Walker (in the early 20th century he ventured into the waterlogged crypt in a diving suit to shore up the foundations) and the chantry chapels of William of Wykeham (bishop and founder of Winchester College). Climb the tower for a rooftop view, and look down at the atmospheric Norman crypt: it floods periodically, but you can look into the bottom of the building and see where it's been shored up. The choir stalls and misericords contain a wealth of wood carving.

The dean and canons live in the Cathedral Close – a delightful area to stroll around, past the arcaded Deanery and ancient Pilgrims Hall (now a prep school). The King's Gate leads out of the close and within moments you're beside Winchester College – one of the oldest public schools of England. The guided tour takes in the quadrangles, Cloister Court, chapel and hall.

Next to the early 18th-century Bishop's Palace is the substantial medieval ruin of Wolvesey Palace, the former bishop's residence – once moated and rising to four storeys. With imagination you can conjure up the opulent lifestyle the bishops must have enjoyed here. The last recorded visit was in 1544 when Queen Mary came here for her marriage to Philip of Spain.

Near the West Gate, by the council offices, once stood the castle, of which virtually nothing remains except the Great Hall. It was Victorianised during its time as a courtroom, when the statue of Queen Victoria was installed. It bears on one wall the Round Table that has been rather spuriously linked with King Arthur. The table is like a dartboard, with names of the 24 Knights of the Round Table around it. It's medieval and was repainted during the time of Henry VIII, but is a great curio anyway.

The Hospital of St Cross, some way out of the centre, still cares for elderly brothers as it has done for over 850 years. The best way to get there is to walk along the water meadows from the centre of town (about 1 mile/1.6 km). Go along College Street, into College Walk and then where the road bends left, take the path on the right through the water meadows; you can also park at St Cross near The Bell pub. St Cross still provides the Wayfarer's Dole – a small mug of beer and a morsel of bread – to those who request it at the porter's lodge. The brothers, in their traditional gowns and trencher hats, act as visitor guides to the medieval hall, the Georgian kitchen, the Tudor cloister and the walled garden.

Butser Ancient Farm

Follow woodland and downland trails to a unique archaeological farmstead, continue through two of Hampshire's oldest and prettiest villages, Chalton and Buriton, and then climb Butser Hill for all-round views.

Route Directions

1 From the car park, follow the Woodland Trail (green-booted posts) to the right. On reaching the road, turn right then left and join the gravelled track at a blue-topped horseshoe post. Follow the waymarked bridleway past the maintenance yard, and bear away from the A3 on to a grassy lane.

2 Gently climb between fields, the bridleway soon curving left around woodland, then gradually bear right between fields, noting the 18th-century windmill on the skyline to your right.

3 At the road, turn right to visit Butser Ancient Farm, otherwise turn left and follow the road (some blind bends) for 0.5 mile (800m) into Chalton. Turn left at the junction, signed 'Ditcham'. (Bear right for the Red Lion.)

4 Shortly, at a fork, bear left along a byway. Continue between fields and soon descend through trees to join a road. Turn left, walking parallel to the railway for 0.25 mile (400m), to a stile on the right. Bear half-left across a large field, pass under electricity lines, and enter woodland.

5 At a junction of paths continue straight ahead and steadily climb a wide forest track. On the descent fork left, then almost immediately fork right, down a narrow sunken footpath and continue down to a road (also the South Downs Way).

6 Turn right then, in 100yds (91m), take the footpath left and head steeply down through the trees to a stile. Bear half right across a field to a stile by a gate then follow the path round to the left, passing a pond, into Buriton.

7 Turn left along the High Street then, beside Chapel Cottage, take the footpath left. Go round the village hall and continue past the play area to a gate. Very carefully cross the railway line, go through a gate and keep ahead to a junction with a bridleway. Turn right and steeply ascend to the road. Cross into Hall's Hill car park.

8 Go through a gate and up a wide track (South Downs Way) back into Queen Elizabeth Country Park. Gradually ascend then, just after a track merges from the right, fork right (signed 'South Downs Way walkers and cyclists'). Keep ahead at the barbecue shelter, and descend past a barrier. Pass through Benham Bushes car park, follow a short stretch of metalled road then bear off left with the South Downs Way. Rejoin the road at Gravel Hill car park and turn right, signed 'Hangers Way', and retrace your outward route to the car park.

Route facts

DISTANCE/TIME 6.75 miles (10.9km) 3h

MAP OS Explorer 120 Chichester

START Pay-and-display car park, Queen Elizabeth Country Park; grid ref: SU 718185

TRACKS Woodland paths, bridleways and forest tracks, 3 stiles.

GETTING TO THE START The Queen Elizabeth Country Park is between Petersfield and Horndean, signposted east off the A3, 3 miles (4.8km) south of Petersfield. The car park is beside the country park's visitor centre.

THE PUB The Five Bells, Buriton. Tel: 01730 263584

❶ Care needed when crossing the railway line; the lane to Chalton can be busy. Two long climbs and a steep ascent into Buriton.

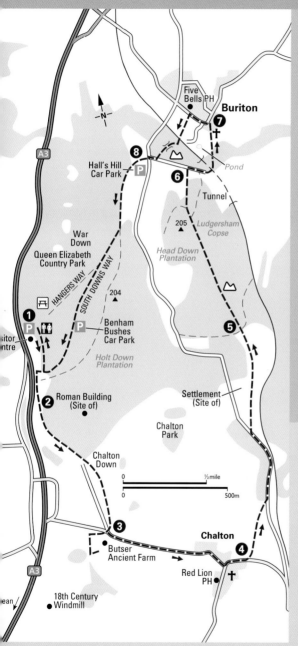

■ TOURIST INFORMATION CENTRES

Alton
7 Cross and Pillory Lane.
Tel: 01420 88448

Petersfield
County Library, 27 The
Square. Tel: 01730 268829

Winchester
Guildhall, High Street.
Tel: 01962 840 500

Hampshire Downs
www.visitwinchester.co.uk

■ PLACES OF INTEREST

Butser Ancient Farm
Petersfield.
Tel: 023 9259 8838; www.
butserancientfarm.co.uk

**Curtis Museum
& Allen Gallery**
High Street, Alton.
Tel: 01420 82802
Local history, ceramics and
the Tichborne spoons.

Gilbert White's House
The Wakes, High Street,
Selborne. Tel: 01420 511275;
www.gilbertwhiteshouse.
org.uk

Hinton Ampner
Tel: 01962 771305;
www.nationaltrust.org.uk

Jane Austen's House
Chawton. Tel: 01420 83262;
www.jane-austens-house-
museum.org.uk

St Cross Hospital
Winchester.
Tel: 01932 851375;
www.stcrosshospital.co.uk

Wickham Vineyard
Botley Road, Shedfield.
Tel: 01329 834042;
www.wickhamvineyard.co.uk

Winchester College
College Street.
Tel: 01962 621209;
www.winchestercollege.co.uk

■ FOR CHILDREN

Fort Nelson
Portsdown Hill.
Tel: 01329 233734;
www.royalarmouries.org
Spectacular 19th-century
fort, forming part of the
Royal Armouries.

Intech
Near Winchester.
Tel: 01962 863791;
www.intech-uk.com
Family-orientated science
centre; science shows.

Marwell Wildlife
Near Winchester.
Tel: 01962 777407;
www.marwell.org.uk

**Mid-Hants Railway
(Watercress Line)**
Tel 01962 733810;
www.watercressline.co.uk

**Queen Elizabeth
Country Park**
Petersfield.
Tel: 023 9259 5040;
www3.hants.gov.uk/qecp

River Park Leisure Centre
Gordon Road,
Winchester.
Tel: 01962 848700; www.
riverparkleisurecentre.co.uk

Winchester Cathedral
www.winchester-cathedral.
org.uk
Tower or roof tours, trails,
brass rubbing and gargoyle
modelling workshops.

■ SHOPPING

Winchester is the region's
major shopping town, with
a high street and some good
individual shops. Alresford
has stylish independent
shops and boutiques.

SELBORNE
The Selborne Gallery
Tel: 01420 511233
The mouth-and-foot painting
artists' gallery.

WINCHESTER
Cadogan & James
31a The Square.
Tel: 01962 877399
A fine delicatessen with a
choice of cheeses and pasta.

Georgie Porgie's
9 Great Minster Street.
Tel: 01962 877871
Stylish clothes and gifts
for children.

The Toy Cupboard
65 St George's Street.
Tel: 01962 849988;
www.thetoycupboard.co.uk
Traditional/educational toys.

Wells Booksellers
11 College Street.
Tel: 01962 852016
The city's oldest bookshop.

MARKETS

Alton

High Street, Tue.

New Alresford,

Broad Street, Thu. Producers Market 1st Sun of month.

Winchester

Antiques Market, Kings Walk, (also regular antiques fairs in the Guildhall).

City Market, Middlebrook Street. Wed–Sat. Everything from food, fruit and vegetables to flowers and secondhand books.

Farmers' Market, Middlebrook Street. The largest in Britain, 2nd and last Sun of month.

■ LOCAL SPECIALITIES

The English Hampshire Lavender Company

Hartley Park Farm (on B3006 north of Selborne). Tel: 01420 511146; www. english-hampshire-lavender. co.uk

Mange2 Deli

44–46 West Street, New Alresford. Tel: 01962 733189 Sells a good range of local cheeses and chocolates.

■ PERFORMING ARTS

Theatre Royal

Jewry Street, Winchester. Tel: 01962 840440; www.theatre-royal-winchester.co.uk

Tower Arts Centre

Romsey Road, Winchester. Tel: 01962 737360; www.towerarts.co.uk Off-the-wall acts.

Grange Park Opera

Grange Park, near New Alresford. Tel: 01962 868888; www.grangeparkopera.co.uk

■ SPORTS & ACTIVITIES

FISHING

Fishing Breaks Ltd

The Mill, Heathman Street, Nether Wallop. Tel: 01264 781988; www.fishingbreaks.co.uk On the Itchen, Arle and around the Test and Avon. Day rods, fly fishing school.

Avington Trout Fishery

Avington, near Winchester. Tel: 01962 779312; www.avingtontrout.com

Meon Springs Fly Fishery

Whitewool Farm, East Meon. Tel: 01730 823134; www.meonsprings.com

Marwell Wildlife Breaks

Game lodge-style Marwell Hotel (Tel: 01962 777681; www.marwellhotel.co.uk) Zoofari Getaway breaks that include entrance to Marwell Wildlife.

Tour of Winchester

Visitor Trail by Wheelchair 1-mile (1.6km) route. Contact the tourist office for details.

■ ANNUAL EVENTS & CUSTOMS

New Alresford

Watercress Festival www.watercress.co.uk 2nd Sun in May. Children's activities, farmers market, celebrity chefs.

Winchester

Hampshire Food Festival www.hampshirefare.co.uk Jul. Culinary events.

Hat Fair www.hatfair.co.uk 1st weekend of Jul, Thu–Sun. The UK's longest-running festival of street theatre. Lots of audience participation – be warned.

Winchester Festival www.winchesterfestival.co.uk Highbrow arts festival, with top names in theatre, literature, visual arts and music. Guided walks. Jul.

ALRESFORD

Tea Rooms

Caracoli
**15 Broad Street, New
Alresford SO24 9AR
Tel: 01962 738730**
With its fresh, modern décor
and courtyard garden, this
coffee shop and food store
is a chic place for a light bite.
Ingredients are carefully
chosen: try their watercress
scones. There's also an array
of preserves, teas, coffees,
chutneys and wines for sale.

Cassandra's Cup
**Winchester Road,
Chawton GU34 1SD
Tel: 01420 83144**
Opposite Jane Austen's
house, and named after her
sister, Cassandra's Cup has
a cheerful interior with floral
plates displayed on a dresser.
Light lunches and tea and
cakes are on offer.

Gilbert White's Tea Parlour
**The Wakes, High Street,
Selborne GU34 3JH
Tel: 01420 511275;
www.gilbertwhiteshouse.
org.uk**
This tea room overlooking the
busy village street is inside
the house of the naturalist
Gilbert White. It makes the
perfect setting to tuck into
scones, light lunches and the
odd dish from an 18th-
century recipe, accompanied
by a range of speciality teas.

Pubs

The Bell Hotel
**12 West Street, New
Alresford SO24 9AT
Tel: 01962 732429;
www.bellalresford.com**
An elegant revamp of an old
inn with pine tables and a
carpeted bar area. Try the
filled baguettes, bar food or
the watercress specialities,
washed down with a good
local brew such as Itchen's
Watercress Line.

Harrow Inn
**Steep GU32 2DA
Tel: 01730 262685**
This unspoiled tile-hung
500-year-old country pub has
two bars furnished simply
with scrubbed wooden tables
and an inglenook. They have
three Hampshire ales and a
guest beer from the cask, as
well as local wine, good ham
and pea soup, cottage pie and
puddings. Children are not
allowed inside, but there's
a large and pleasant garden.

Hotel du Vin
**Southgate Street,
Winchester SO23 9EF
Tel: 01962 841414;
www.hotelduvin.com**
The bistro of this Georgian
hotel in the city centre makes
an excellent if pricey stop for
lunch or coffee. There's a
stylish champagne bar and a
pretty walled courtyard. Food
has a French leaning, and
dishes might include local
trout or watercress.

Thomas Lord
**High Street,
West Meon GU32 1LN
Tel: 01730 829244;
www.thethomaslord.co.uk**
Relaxed and friendly, this
welcoming old village pub
has a nicely rustic interior
with an eclectic range of old
furniture, open fires and an
interesting selection of real
ales. The food is served in
generous portions, and they
grow some of their own
produce. If the weather is
fine, the garden is an
attractive setting for a pint.

Wykeham Arms
**75 Kingsgate Street,
Winchester SO23 9PE
Tel: 01962 854411**
A fine historic pub right in the
middle of things, this has
fascinating décor: old college
desks and collections of
walking sticks, pictures,
tankards and Winchester
College caps. The food is
varied and inspiring, with
anything from sandwiches
upwards; it's more elaborate
in the evening. No children.

Chichester & Arundel

There's a bewitchingly secretive quality to the South Downs here, with dense woodlands cloaking the slopes above the yacht-filled watery inlets of Chichester Harbour, and thatched villages nestled beneath. It's long been an area favoured by the seriously rich: Fishbourne Roman Palace, Petworth House, Parham, Goodwood, Uppark and Arundel Castle speak volumes about the moneyed classes. Sussex's two great outdoor museums at Amberley and Singleton evoke the regional life of yesteryear.

3 Walk start point

1 Tour start point

Unmissable attractions

Get close to magnificent mosaics at Fishbourne and Bignor, two of Britain's greatest Roman villa sites...encounter the living past at Amberley Working Museum and the Weald and Downland Open-Air Museum...home in on the rich bird life at the Arundel Wetland Centre as you glide through the reeds on an electric craft...take a boat trip round Chichester Harbour from West Itchenor or picnic among the dunes at East Head...admire the modern British art at Chichester's Pallant House and the Cass Sculpture Foundation at Goodwood House...maybe have a little flutter on the horses at Glorious Goodwood...catch a glimpse of the nobility's lifestyle at Petworth House and Arundel Castle...wander the eerie forest of ancient yews at Kingley Vale.

1 Weald & Downland Open-Air Museum

Historic buildings have been rescued from destruction and rebuilt here to evoke country life and show local building styles.

2 Petworth House & Park

Set in a 700-acre (284ha) deer park landscaped by 'Capability' Brown, Petworth is an impressive 17th-century mansion with the greatest art collection held by any National Trust property.

3 Pagham Harbour Nature Reserve

This undeveloped landscape of low lying saltmarsh, mudflats and shingle shore attracts many species of waders and wildfowl.

4 Arundel Castle

Set high on a hill, magnificent Arundel Castle, the ancestral home of the Dukes of Norfolk, commands stunning views across the River Arun and out to sea.

5 Chichester

Chichester's vast natural harbour, a designated Area of Outstanding Natural Beauty, is a popular sailing centre, and its channels offer a safe mooring for all types of cruising vessels.

6 Fishbourne Roman Palace

One of Britain's most splendid and important Roman sites, Fishbourne was occupied from the 1st to the 3rd centuries AD.

■ Activity

WALKS ON THE SOUTH DOWNS WAY

Easily followed, and waymarked with distinctive acorn motifs, the long-distance South Downs Way takes in some of the finest scenery in the region. Highlights of the route that make rewarding strolls in this area include:

The Harting Downs (entry from a car park by the B2141 just southeast of South Harting), with easy access on to Beacon Hill, with its Iron Age ramparts, and a huge view over the Weald. The chalk grassland here is a designated nature reserve, with characteristic wild flowers.

The Downs above Storrington and Amberley, easily reached by two dead-end roads that climb up to the crest (Chantry Lane, from the A283 at Storrington) and another road rising from the B2139. It is very open on top, a strong contrast from the wooded sections further west.

AMBERLEY MAP REF TQ0314

With its many thatched houses and idyllic position by water meadows, this village presents a picture of rare perfection. A 10-minute walk from the rail station, it has plenty to fill a day, with walks on to the downs and along the River Arun, and an outstanding industrial museum. There's a view of the extremely imposing curtain wall of the medieval castle (now a smart hotel) from its north side if you walk down to the edge of the village from where the great wetland of Amberley Wild Brooks spreads. This is an area of water meadows that's now managed as a nature reserve by the Sussex Wildlife Trust and is a prized habitat for dragonflies and, during winter flooding, various wildfowl such as

Bewick's swans. A footpath from the village penetrates the reserve and provides a beautiful walk at any time of year, floods allowing, to Greatham Bridge – a multi-arched stone bridge dating from the 16th century and joined to a metal span over the River Arun. Water meadows like these were created with ditches and sluices, which were deliberately flooded in winter to enrich the farmland with silt. There are river trips to here from Arundel during the summer. On a minor road east of the village, the Sportsman's Arms has a view over Amberley Wild Brooks, and is a pleasant spot for a drink or a meal.

Amberley Museum, just outside the village itself and next to Amberley station, is a stimulating open-air industrial museum in a disused chalk pit, with a series of buildings that include a foundry and an old telephone exchange, a collection of vintage Southdown buses, resident craftspeople (such as a printer, a potter and a clay-pipe maker), and outdoor displays celebrating the industrial heritage and crafts skills of the southeast. Run by volunteers, it succeeds in bringing the region's working past to life, and there's a lively calendar of events too.

ARUNDEL MAP REF TQ0207

The massive castle seems to throw a canopy of living history over Arundel. It was restored and is still occupied by the Dukes of Norfolk, whose ancestors have owned it since 1138. The castle's grounds take up half the hill on which the compact town sits, and you might feel almost on your knees yourself as you approach up steepening pathways. Today, however, you can visit the castle and explore Arundel's other attractions – enjoyable small shops in the historic centre, a spectacular Victorian cathedral in the French Gothic style and more echoes of France in the shady avenue of Mill Road, popular for parking and picnicking and close to the starting point for river trips to Amberley and the Black Rabbit pub. Beyond here is the Arundel Wetland Centre, enjoyable for its setting, its remarkable bird life and wild flowers.

Arundel's sloping, tapered square with its attractive cobbles and simple war memorial is surrounded by a smart group of individual-looking businesses – Pallant's delicatessen, a proper butcher, a gallery and a second-hand book shop. Tarrant Street, running off the High Street, has artisan and specialist shops, some in converted Victorian industrial buildings, such as the Old Print Works. There's a needlework shop, a picture restorers and the Walking Stick Shop. Peglers, expedition advisers and suppliers, has two of its four Arundel shops here and claims to have one of the largest stocks of walking boots in the UK. Further uphill, Maltravers Street is an elegant mix of 18th-century town houses, with the road running on two levels. On the High Street, between Tarrant and Maltravers Street, is the Tourist Information Centre (offering a town audio tour). Nearby Arundel Ghost Experience, in the Old Town Hall, is likely to chill spines of all ages with its ghost stories and sinister prison cells. The volunteer-run local museum is in a temporary hut in Mill Road car park.

Clustered at the top of town, beyond the pedestrian entrance to the castle, is a remarkable collection of religious buildings that could be said to embody Arundel's extraordinary religious history. St Nicholas', Arundel's 14th-century Church of England parish church, backs on to the Fitzalan Chapel (access via the castle grounds), bought by the castle when Henry VIII dissolved its religious foundation and, remarkably, to this day still Catholic: you can see it behind a glass wall beyond St Nicholas' altar. Cromwellian forces used the chapel to stable their horses in the Civil War; it was carefully restored in Victorian times

■ Visit

ARUNDEL WETLAND CENTRE

One of the UK's network of wildfowl and wetland centres established by Sir Peter Scott, the 60 acres (24ha) of ponds, lakes and reeds provide a secure wetland home for hundreds of native creature and plant species, as well as the original collection of waterfowl from across the world. Activities include pond-dipping, family days and art workshops. The Water's Edge restaurant has lakeside viewing, and level paths and boardwalks (wheelchairs available) pass waterfowl enclosures, hides and a camera obscura in thatch. A trip on one of the silent electric boats is a special treat and you don't need to be an expert to enjoy the visit: it's easy to spot the birds and there's something to see at every season. Bird plumage is at its best in spring, the young birds are born in late spring/early summer, late summer is a good time to visit for dragonflies, butterflies and wetland plants such as purple loosestrife and St John's wort, while the autumn and winter see many visiting migrant birds.

and houses the medieval, Tudor and later monuments of a succession of Earls of Arundel and Dukes of Norfolk. The skeletal decomposing cadaver sculpted beneath the effigy of the 7th Earl (died 1435) serves as a reminder of man's mortality. Almost opposite soars Arundel Cathedral, completed in 1873 by the 15th Duke of Norfolk to celebrate Britain's mid-Victorian Catholic revival. It is an almost perfect-looking re-creation of the French Gothic style of about 1400, with strongly vertical lines in honey-coloured Bath stone, scrolly decorations on the skyline, flying buttresses and great rose window. The architect, Joseph Hansom, is perhaps best known for inventing the Hansom Cab. Inside the building, on the right, a stained-glass window depicts the Earl of Arundel, Philip Howard, who was made a saint in 1970, alongside his faithful wife and dog. A member of Court, who rediscovered his Catholic faith, he died after 11 years in the Tower of London under Elizabeth I.

Arundel Castle is a film-maker's dream: its handsome sheer grey walls and battlemented turrets appeared in *The Madness of King George* (1994), where it stood in for Windsor Castle, and *Robin Hood, Prince of Thieves* (1991), and may even have inspired Mervyn Peake's Gormenghast series of fantasy novels. Despite the extensive restorations – it was one of the first great houses to be fitted with electric lights, in the 1890s – it succeeds in giving a good impression of what entering the castle gates of the country's most powerful Duke might have felt like in previous centuries. Low, dimly lit vaulted entrance halls adorned with taxidermy, weaponry and armour make the visitor feel very small, and the massive scale of the Baron's Hall will make you feel smaller still.

The oldest part of the building is the keep, reached by many narrow steps, which has tableaux bringing the Civil War siege to life – this only ended when the Parliamentarian besiegers were able to cut off the castle's water supply. Portcullis mechanisms are on view, and there are tremendous panoramas over the town, cathedral, coastal plain and Downs beyond. Of the occupied rooms on show, the Regency Gothic library is perhaps the finest, with its exuberant gilt balconies and plush red velvet sofas. Elsewhere, the paintings of Van Dyck, Canaletto, Constable and Turner can be found hanging almost casually among hundreds of other works of art, and photographs of the ducal family meeting VIPs such as popes and royalty decorate the tabletops. Prepare to be impressed.

Outside, near the Fitzalan Chapel, a tea terrace set in beautiful gardens looks out straight across to Arundel's French Gothic-style cathedral built in 1873.

■ Visit

DENMANS GARDEN

A short way east of Chichester, this garden packs a good deal into 4 acres (1.6ha). The style is definitely naturalistic and deliberately unmanicured, with the grass allowed to grow long, dotted with statues. The whole place is a burst of colour and texture of flowers and foliage – well worth seeing in autumn as well as in the warmer months, when tulips and flowering shrubs make a magnificent show. There are plenty of seating areas.

There's free access to the network of footpaths in the extensive park, which spreads over the Downs and features a large landscaped lake.

BIGNOR MAP REF SU9815

Tucked in deep countryside beneath a lushly wooded stretch of downs, Bignor village's square of streets boasts some marvellously unchanged old houses, including the Yeoman's House (or Old Shop), a thatched and half-timbered 15th-century cottage with an attractive overhanging upper storey.

Bignor is best known for its Roman villa. It's rather confusing at first sight, as what you see is a set of rustic-looking thatched buildings. These buildings are the shelters, which themselves have become historic structures, put up to protect the Roman remains in the early 19th century by John Hawkins, the landowner. He had the site excavated and transformed it into an early tourist attraction after it was discovered by a ploughman. The same family runs the site today. Inside you can view some of the finest Roman mosaics in Britain, depicting glorious scenes from the lives of gladiators and mythical subjects such as Ganymede being abducted by an eagle, and in places you can even walk on the still-durable surface of a Roman floor. The buildings were added to over the course of a couple of centuries and what survives above ground is mainly from the 4th century AD. There's a full-scale bath suite with a cold plunge pool and a heated changing room, warm and hot rooms and hot bath, which slaves would have stoked up from the outside.

■ Activity

WALK ON STANE STREET ROMAN ROAD

One of the most evocative stretches of Roman road in southern England is on the South Downs. Much of Stane Street, which ran from London to Chichester, is now main road, but you can walk its straight course close to Bignor Roman Villa along a clear man-made ridge, or agger, and in places you can make out the original flint surface (where the turf has been removed by generations of rabbits).

With the villa entrance on the right, drive along the road and fork left at the first junction (where the right turn is signposted Sutton). Immediately turn left by a thatched barn and follow this narrow lane up to the top of the South Downs – ignore the minor left fork half-way up. The car park is at the end of the road. There's a mock Roman signpost pointing to towns with their Roman names like 'Londinium' at the top. The downs here are heavily wooded, but where views do open up you can see far across the woods and farmland of the Weald to the north.

The discovery of Bignor transformed scholars' perceptions of Roman Britain – it was among the earliest evidence for Roman-style 'civilised' living to be found in the countryside. Since then, many other villas have been discovered across southern England, usually in the same kind of open position with a fine view. Most were probably the hubs of large farms serving nearby major cities like Chichester, and the occupants were probably extended families descended from local Iron Age chieftains who had prospered under the Romans, rather than Romans from Italy.

A South Downs circuit from Stoughton

This remote downland landscape is cloaked with 30,000 yew trees covering more than 200 acres (81ha). Kingley Vale became one of Britain's first nature reserves in 1952 and is today managed by English Heritage. Silent and inaccessible by car, it is a haven for ramblers and naturalists. This walk skirts the forest of large squat yew trees, their branches and dark green needles creating a dense evergreen canopy which allows little light to filter to the forest floor. The vale positively teems with wildlife, and rare green woodpeckers are just one of 57 species of bird that breed here. The bee orchid blooms in June, and fallow deer thoughtfully keep the turf cropped short for other species of wild flower to flourish.

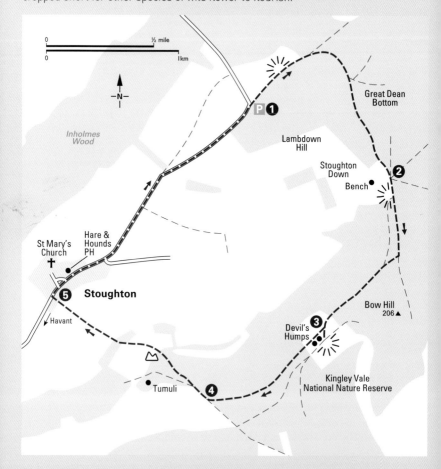

Route Directions

1 Take the bridleway, signposted from the car park entrance, leading away from the road and through a metal barrier, skirting dense woodland. There are striking views on the left over pastoral, well-wooded countryside. Keep right at a fork and follow the stony path as it curves to the right. Veer slightly right, as signposted at the next waymarked fork, and begin a gradual ascent beneath the boughs of beech and oak trees.

2 Eventually you break cover from the trees at a major junction of waymarked tracks. Go straight on, looking to the right for spectacular views. After 125yds (114m), fork left at the next bridleway sign and join a path running parallel to the track. Cut between trees and keep going for 0.25 mile (400m) until you reach a waymarker post. Fork right here. Keep to the waymarked path as it runs down the slope. Rejoin the stony track, turning left to follow it up the slope towards Bow Hill.

3 On reaching the Devil's Humps, veer off the path by a sign for Kingley Vale Nature Reserve to enjoy the magnificent vistas across the downland countryside. The view to the north, over remote woodland and downland, is impressive enough, but the panorama to the south is particularly outstanding. Immediately below you are the trees of Kingley Vale. Return to the nature reserve sign and continue the previous direction along the track, keeping to the right of the Devil's Hump and re-entering the forest.

4 Turn right at the next main junction and follow the bridle track along the field-edge. On the left are glimpses of Chichester Harbour, with its complex network of watery channels and sprawling mudflats, and the Isle of Wight beyond. Pass several ancient burial tumuli and then descend through an area of mixed woodland. Keep going until you reach the road, turn right and walk through the pleasant village of Stoughton.

5 Pass the entrance to St Mary's Church on the left, followed by the Hare and Hounds pub. Continue through the village and on the right is the Monarch's Way. Follow the road out of Stoughton, all the way to the left-hand bend where you'll see the entrance to the car park on Stoughton Down on the right.

Route facts

DISTANCE/TIME 5 miles (8km) 2h

MAP OS Explorer 120 Chichester, South Harting & Selsey

START Free car park at Stoughton Down (8am–dusk); grid ref: SZ 814125

TRACKS Mostly woodland paths and downland tracks.

GETTING TO THE START Stoughton is situated between Petersfield and Chichester, signed 2 miles (3.2km) east off the B2146. Pass through Walderton and Stoughton village and the car park at Stoughton Down is 1 mile (1.6km) further on.

THE PUB Hare & Hounds, Stoughton. Tel: 023 9263 1433

❶ Care needed on the country lanes out of Stoughton. Ascents and descents gentle but long.

Meandering in and around Midhurst

This easy town and country stroll follows the pretty River Rother to the ruins of Cowdray House. There is plenty to see on the walk as Midhurst has many splendid buildings, including the famous tile-hung library, the old chemist's shop and the grammar school where H G Wells taught. When you leave Midhurst you head for wooded countryside. It's not long, though, before you are returning to the pleasant environs of the town, following a path through the woods above the River Rother. One of the highlights of the walk is to step between the trees on the right to look down at the river and across to Cowdray House, the ruins of which opened to the public as a tourist attraction in the spring of 2007.

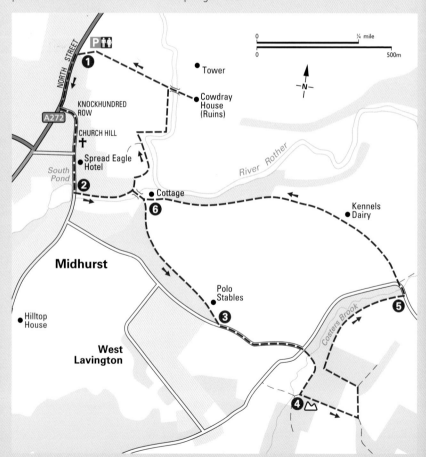

Route Directions

1 From the car park by the tourist information centre turn left and walk along North Street, passing the post office. Bear left into Knockhundred Row. Walk along Church Hill and into South Street to pass along the side of the historic Spread Eagle Hotel.

2 Turn left by South Pond into The Wharf, following a bridleway beside industrial buildings and flats. Trees on the right enclose a stream. Bear right at the next waymarked junction, cross the bridge and pass a cottage on the left. Keep the wooden fencing on the right and avoid the path running off to the left. Make for a stile, then continue ahead along the edge of fields, keeping trees and vegetation on the right. Cross two stiles and follow the path to the right of the polo stables.

3 Keep left and follow a pleasantly wooded stretch of road. Pass some pretty cottages and on reaching a bend join a bridle path signposted 'Heyshott and Graffham'. Follow the track as it curves to the right.

4 Veer left just before the entrance to a house and follow the waymarked path as it climbs quite steeply through the trees, passing between woodland glades and carpets of bracken. Drop down the slope to a waymarked path junction and turn left to join a sandy track. Keep left at the fork and follow the track as it bends sharply to the right.

5 On reaching the road, turn left and, when it bends left by some gates, go straight on along the bridleway towards Kennels Dairy. Keep to the left of the outbuildings and stable blocks and walk ahead to several galvanised gates. Continue on the path and when it reaches a field gateway, go through the gate to the right of it, following the path as it runs just inside the woodland.

6 Continue along to the junction forming part of the outward leg of the walk, turn right and retrace your steps to the bridge. Avoid the path on the left, running along to South Pond, and veer over to the right to rejoin the river bank. Keep going until you reach a footpath on the left, leading up to the ruins of St Ann's Hill. Follow the path beside the Rother, heading for a kissing gate. Turn left and make for a bridge which provides access to Cowdray House. After visiting the house, go straight ahead along the causeway path to the car park.

Route facts

DISTANCE/TIME 3 miles (4.8km) 2h

MAP OS Explorer 120 Chichester, South Harting & Selsey

START Free car park by the tourist information centre, North Street, Midhurst; grid ref: SZ 886217

TRACKS Pavements, field, riverside tracks and country road, 4 stiles.

GETTING TO THE START Midhurst is on the A272 midway between Petersfield and Petworth. The car park is on North Street as you head out of the town on the A272 toward Petworth.

THE PUB The Angel Hotel, Midhurst. Tel: 01730 812421

❶ Care needed walking through the town and along the riverside paths. One fairly steep ascent, which can be slippery when wet.

CHICHESTER MAP REF SU8604

With some 20,000 students at its college and university, and as the home of one of the biggest summer arts festivals on the south coast as well as the renowned Chichester Festival Theatre, Chichester positively buzzes with life and activity. Encircled by town walls that date from Roman times it's a delightful place, with a regular medieval crisscross of mostly pedestrianised streets at the heart of its historic centre, and an impressive range of independent shops and high street chains all within strolling distance. The centre is further encircled by a rather forbidding inner ring road (via which you'll find the main car parks; one of the cheapest is Avenue de Chartres, near the rail station), once you're away from that the city's charms become evident.

A Market Cross bristling with ornate pinnacles and pennants was given to Chichester in 1501 by Bishop Edward Story as a central place for produce vendors to congregate. It stands at the meeting of West, North, East and South Streets. With this compass orientation to get you started, it's an easy place to get to grips with. Along North Street are the red-brick Council House, with its Roman inscribed stone set behind glass in one wall, and the colonnaded Market House of 1807, designed by John Nash and still filled with market stalls.

Just west of the Market Cross is the cathedral, its spire visible from miles around across the pancake-flat coastal plain and from the Downs. Britain's only detached cathedral bell tower stands in front, and in summer doubles as the box office for the Chichester Festivities, the city's big arts event. The interior is a harmonious mixture of ancient and modern. Its roof is a supreme example of stone vaulting, introduced after fire devastated the wooden roof in 1184, while striking 20th-century additions are Marc Chagall's window of Creation (1978) and John Piper's tapestry (1966). Of the building's many splendid monuments, none is more touching than the Arundel Tomb of a 14th-century stone knight (Earl Fitzalan) and his lady, actually holding hands. Look too for the stone panel of Lazarus at Bethany, a masterpiece of early medieval sculpture.

The cathedral was never actually a monastery, and the cloisters are just passageways around what was the burial ground. Behind spread the precincts: the Bishop's Palace (still the bishop's residence) lies at the end of Canon Lane, itself spanned by the gateway, and off here is Vicars Close, four cottages with flower-filled gardens. The Bishop's Palace Gardens is a secretive place with picnic spots peeping over red-brick walls and through gates to the cathedral.

Between South and East Streets lies Chichester's Georgian quarter, divided into four streets – North, West, South and East Pallant – like the city's street layout in miniature. The Pallant House Gallery here is known as the foremost museum of modern art in Sussex.

Due to move from Little London to new premises in Tower Street during 2011, Chichester District Museum has absorbing displays from its archaeology, geology and local history collection. The museum also arranges guided walks in the Chichester district at weekends.

Around the Arun Valley from Arundel

Follow the River Arun to Arundel Park and then tour this handsome Sussex town, dominated by its massive castle. The walk starts down by the River Arun and from here there are teasing glimpses of the castle, but it is not until you have almost finished the walk that you reach its main entrance. Following the river bank through the tranquil Arun valley, the walk reaches Arundel Park. Swanbourne Lake, a great attraction for young children, is located by the entrance to the park, but beyond here the park assumes a rather different character. You may start to feel slightly isolated at this point but don't worry; resume the walk and you will soon be back in the hustle and bustle of Arundel's busy streets.

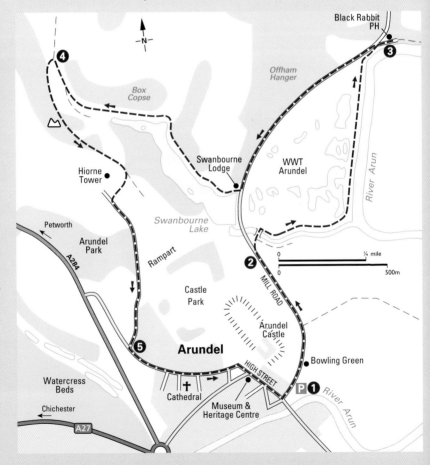

Route Directions

1 From the car park in Mill Road, turn right and walk along the tree-lined pavement. Pass the bowling green and a glance to your left will reveal a dramatic view of historic Arundel Castle with its imposing battlements.

2 Follow the road to the elegant stone bridge, avoid the first path on the right and cross over via a footbridge and turn right to join the riverside path, partly shaded by overhanging trees. Emerging from the trees, the path cuts across lush, low-lying ground to reach the western bank of the Arun. Turn left here and walk beside the reed-fringed Arun to the Black Rabbit pub, which can be seen standing out against a curtain of trees.

3 From the Black Rabbit, turn left on the minor road back towards Arundel, passing the entrance to the WWT Arundel Wetland Centre. Make for the gate leading into Arundel Park and follow the path alongside Swanbourne Lake. Eventually the lake fades from view as the walk reaches deeper into the park. Ignore a turning branching off to the left, just before a gate and stile, and follow the path as it curves gently to the right.

4 Turn sharply to the left at the next waymarked junction and begin a fairly steep ascent, with the footpath through the park seen curving away down to the left, back towards the lake. This stretch of the walk offers glorious views over elegant Arundel Park. Head for a stile and gate, then bear immediately right up the bank. Cross the grass, following the waymarks and keeping to the left of Hiorne Tower. On reaching a driveway, turn left and walk down to Park Lodge. Keep to the right by the private drive and make for the road.

5 Turn left, pass Arundel Cathedral and bear left at the road junction by the entrance to Arundel Castle. Go down the hill, back into the centre of Arundel. You'll find Mill Road at the bottom of the High Street.

Route facts

DISTANCE/TIME 3.25 miles (5.3km) 2h

MAP OS Explorer 121 Arundel & Pulborough

START Fee-paying car park, Mill Road, Arundel; grid ref: TQ 020071

TRACKS Riverside and parkland paths, some road walking, 2 stiles.

GETTING TO THE START Arundel is located just off the A27 between Chichester and Worthing, 10 miles (16.1km) east of Chichester. If heading west on the A27, exit for the town centre at the first roundabout. Cross the River Arun and turn right into Mill Road. The car park is 100yds (91m) along on the right.

THE PUB Black Rabbit, Offham. Tel: 01903 882828

❶ Section of road with no pavement (generally light traffic). Arundel Park is closed annually on 24 March. Dogs are not permitted in Arundel Park.

CHICHESTER HARBOUR
MAP REF SU7600

Flat farmlands, saltmarshes and mudflats surround this vast natural harbour, where thousands of bobbing masts attest to its status as one of the major yachting havens of the south coast. A series of inlets and peninsulas make it into a complicated, watery landscape with constantly changing views: there are footpaths along parts of the shore, but the best way to see this natural wonder is from the water itself.

From West Itchenor, Chichester Harbour Water Tours give 1.5-hour cruises on the harbour up to five times a day – with the chance to spot birds such as shelducks, teals and mergansers, as well as seals. Surfers head towards East Wittering and Bracklesham Bay when the conditions are right. On warm summer days it gets very busy at West Wittering, but the crowds soon thin out as you venture on to East Head, a spit of land jutting into Chichester Harbour with a short but scenic walk around it.

■ Visit

PAGHAM HARBOUR

Bring a pair of binoculars for this prime site for wildfowl and waders, a 1,450-acre (587ha) nature reserve belonging to the Sussex Wildlife Trust. It's a body of almost landlocked water tucked away near Selsey Bill. The shingle, saltmarsh, copses, lagoons and reedbeds attract dunlins, grey plovers, curlews and Brent geese. Park by the 13th-century church at the old part of Pagham village and walk along the inland side of the water along a raised dyke. Just over a mile (1.6km) away the path reaches a well-placed pub, the Crab and Lobster.

FISHBOURNE MAP REF SU8405

On the western fringes of Chichester are found the remains of the largest Roman building yet discovered north of the Alps. No ordinary Roman villa, it is a huge complex with some 100 rooms and 60 mosaics, believed to be unique in Britain and more on the scale of an emperor's palace in Rome. Revealed in 1960 when workmen began laying a water main, Fishbourne Roman Palace has since become one of the most celebrated archaeological excavations of its time. One theory is that the Romans built it as a reward for a local king, Togidubnus, in return for his providing support and a safe harbour during their 43 AD invasion.

Inside, orientate yourself by looking at the model of the whole palace. What you see now is only one side of a great quadrangle – the rest lies beneath the road and houses of Fishbourne village. Helpfully, the audio-visual show has a virtual reality reconstruction.

In the recently refurbished main shelter building, walkways take visitors above the mosaics, allowing an excellent view. The mosaics vary in design – the earliest have simple black-and-white geometric patterns – and some of them seem to be draped over lumpy surfaces where they were built over ditches and pits and have since subsided. The Cupid on a Dolphin mosaic, a remarkable piece of art, is the finest and the most famous: the head of Medusa has some decidedly wobbly borders which have been attributed to inexperienced local craftsmen of the time.

Outside, the box hedges are planted in the same intricate patterns as the

Roman bedding trenches uncovered by the excavation, and across the garden there's an exhibit on Roman gardening with a range of tools on display.

Back across the car park, the impressive Collections Discovery Centre deals with the conservation methods and storage of archaeological 'finds' (tours available). There's a good-value café, and grassy slopes for picnicking. Look out for special events that are held throughout the year. There are themed weekends with Roman re-enactments and craft demonstrations, and theatre performances. The Chichester–Bosham cycle path runs behind the site and you can hire bikes in Fishbourne village.

KINGLEY VALE NATIONAL NATURE RESERVE
MAP REF SU8310

Yew forests are extremely rare, and this one, found on the South Downs between Stoughton and West Stoke – is Europe's largest, although tests involving pollen analysis suggest there were yew forests elsewhere in the area during prehistoric times, as at Mount Caburn near Lewes. It's a marvellously eerie place, like some Tolkienesque fantasy, which is at its most spectacularly creepy and magical in the yew grove. Follow the path from the car park near West Stoke, keep forward at the next path junction, then go through a gate, to join the circular nature trail. Gnarled tree trunks have fallen over or twisted and continued to grow, creating a dark, gloomy canopy under which little else thrives. The luscious-looking berries are poisonous to us, but not to the hungry birds such as

nuthatches, goldcrests and thrushes which feed on them. As you reach the top, the view opens out dramatically across Chichester Harbour – with the spire of Chichester Cathedral in view. The tall grassy mounds up here are burial mounds consisting of a mound and ditch (or 'bell barrows') erected in the Bronze Age, doubtless for the view.

MIDHURST MAP REF SU8922

There is almost nothing out of place in Midhurst, a market town that feels more like a village: timber-framed pubs overhang little back streets; Boots has an early black-and-gold shop front with curly lettering and bow windows. The author H G Wells lodged at Ye Olde Tea Shoppe, and he studied and taught at Midhurst Grammar School. The public library is a quaint tile-hung cottage, with a huge mounting block outside. In the curiously named Knockhundred Row, the Market has antiques shops and bookshops, while Harveys of Lewes has its second brewery shop in a 15th-century building in Red Lion Street. A short walk from the car park by the Tourist Information Centre brings you to the Cowdray Ruins, a Tudor mansion that burned down in 1793 and became a 'romantic' tourist attraction whose battlemented turrets and stone mullioned windows were admired by Turner and others. Recent conservation has stabilised the fragile structure and provided a visitor centre in the nearby stables. Just beyond are the lawns of the Cowdray Park Polo Club. Outside town to the northwest, Woolbeding Common is a hilly heathland with picnic places.

PARHAM MAP REF TQ0714

This stately mansion, which is essentially an Elizabethan house, is set in superb gardens in a great deer park beneath the Downs. The Great Hall is half panelled with mullion windows reaching right up to the ceiling, affording glorious views of the Downs, and plasterwork pendants on the ceiling. The other rooms are more intimate – the Great Parlour has a low ceiling and ticking clocks and leads into the Saloon, decorated in the classical style in the 18th century. Upstairs, the Great Chamber has a four-poster bed, with examples of early needlework: the flame stitch on the bed canopy exterior dates from about 1620, while the French or Italian work on the inner hangings is from c1585. The Long Gallery displays a miscellany of objects that includes a Georgian barrel organ and a sedan chair.

You can glimpse the house and visit the estate church from a footpath that crosses the estate from Amberley along the Downs, through Parham Park and back through the Wild Brooks.

PETWORTH MAP REF SU9822

The town is dominated by the 17th-century Petworth House – its upper windows peering over near the church, and its great wall squeezing the A272 traffic uncomfortably close to the town's fine stone, half-timbered and tile-hung buildings. Shops are scattered all around the streets near the square, some dotted along picturesquely cobbled Lombard Street. Petworth Cottage Museum at 346 High Street, takes you back to 1910 when Mary Cummings, seamstress of Petworth House, lived there.

Petworth House (National Trust) can be reached on foot via an entrance near the church, or from a car park north of the town. Another car park located a mile (1.6km) or so to the north gives free access to the grounds, where cyclists are welcomed. The hilly parkland here represents 18th-century landscaping by the great 'Capability' Brown on a huge scale, set against which the house itself seems oddly restrained. Its flat classical frontage in creamy grey stone seems a little sunken into the ground and the pasture goes right up to the windows.

Inside, the main rooms of the house have immensely different characters, from the gilt mirrors and oil paintings in the Square Drawing Room to the Marble Hall with its black-and-white floor, cool sage-green paint and authentic Roman statuary. One highlight is the Carved Room, decorated in c1692 by Grinling Gibbons and the Petworth carpenter John Selden, with astonishing carvings in limewood. Festoons of flowers, beads, birds, musical instruments, cherubs and lace are created in three dimensions, and tend to rather upstage the four Turner landscapes which hang beneath Tudor family and royal portraits.

The art here is the finest of any National Trust House; the North Wing Gallery includes works by Turner (a regular guest here) as well as Blake, Bosch, Titian and Gainsborough.

As you leave the house you get a glimpse of the medieval manor around which it was constructed. Opposite are found the servants' quarters, which now display the late Victorian kitchens and house the high-ceilinged tea room.

Petworth and Amberley

This tour makes the most of the bewitching scenery of the West Sussex Downs, with glimpses of the distant sea. You can visit Petworth House and Uppark (both National Trust properties), or venture into Europe's largest yew forest at Kingley Vale, and see some of England's finest Roman mosaics at Bignor Roman Villa. Learn about the region's traditional building styles at the Weald and Downland Open Air Museum, and find out about the working life of yesteryear in Amberley Working Museum.

Route Directions

Start the drive at Petworth, where the estate walls of Petworth House extend to the town centre. This house has the finest art collection of any National Trust property, and in addition to its stately rooms, has a huge deer park.

1 Take the A272 west through Easebourne to Midhurst. Midhurst's beautifully preserved town centre around the church is worth exploring.

2 Leave Midhurst by the A272 towards Petersfield. Leave the A272 near Stedham, turning left on a minor road through Elsted (where the delightfully placed Three Horseshoes makes a very pleasant stop) to turn left through South Harting. South Harting was the home of Anthony Trollope, the novelist, and has an attractive sloping village street.

3 Fork right on to the B2146. You will soon pass the entrance to Uppark.

This supremely elegant classical mansion suffered a huge fire in 1989 and the National Trust painstakingly restored it to what it was before the disaster. At West Marden you can divert right to Stansted House, a Georgian mansion in a great park, while at Walderton you can detour left to Stoughton.

4 Beyond Walderton, turn left to stay on the B2146, then take the B2178 towards Chichester and, at East Ashling, turn left and continue following the National Nature Reserve signposts. At North Stoke, a car park gives access to Kingley Vale National Nature Reserve. Follow the path from the car park, and at a path junction go ahead through a gate to follow the circular nature trail through the magical yew grove of Kingley Vale and up to the crest of the Downs, where Bronze Age burial mounds known as 'bell barrows' look over Chichester Harbour.

5 Continue east and turn left on the A286 at Mid Lavant. At West Dean are West Dean Gardens, in the grounds of a prestigious arts college, beautifully set along the River Lavant and looking up to the Downs. Very close by is the Weald and Downland Museum, where traditionally constructed buildings from all over southeast England have been re-erected. You can eat at the museum's café, or seek out the Partridge, a cottagey village pub with a garden in Singleton.

6 Turn right off the A286, beyond West Dean, following the road up to Goodwood racecourse, and fork left towards Petworth. Beyond 'Glorious Goodwood' you can see the sea at Bognor Regis. Selhurst Park, by the road on the left, is a forest area with fine views.

7 Turn left on the A285 towards Petworth. After 3.6 miles (5.8km), just where the

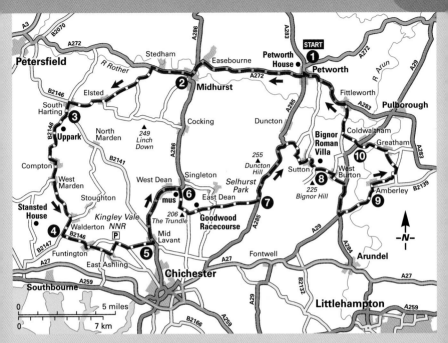

road drops from the Downs, turn right at the bottom of the hill on a lane through Sutton to Bignor Roman Villa. The villa contains magnificent mosaics and has been a tourist attraction since its chance discovery by a ploughman in 1811. You can also divert up on to the South Downs on a little lane ending on Bignor Hill, and explore Stane Street, a dead straight Roman road now demoted to a track, but well preserved with its agger (ditch) still visible alongside.

8 Carry on through West Burton to Bury. Turn right on the A29, then take the B2139 at the roundabout. You pass the Amberley Working Museum, set in a chalk pit, and home to a community of craftspeople and re-erected buildings recalling working life in the southeast of England.

9 Turn left into the beautiful village of Amberley, with its many thatched houses and the castle overlooking the water meadows. Follow the road that bends right by the Black Horse in Amberley village, and keep left at two junctions to the village of Greatham.

Greatham Bridge is an idyllic place to sit and relax beside the River Arun.

10 Cross the A29 at Coldwaltham, and turn right on the B2138 to Fittleworth, where the unusual pub sign for the Swan spans the road. Turn left on the A283 and continue to Petworth.

A Downland Ramble at Amberley

This interesting walk allows you to re-create the charm of England's rustic past with a fascinating visit to a working museum before you stretch your legs and expand your lungs by climbing high on to the Downs. Amberley is a charming thatched village with a history stretching back to medieval times and was the summer residence of the Bishops of Chichester. It may sound strange, but this invigorating downland walk begins where reality meets nostalgia. By visiting an old chalk quarry at the start of the route, you have the chance to forget – however briefly – the hurly-burly of the modern world. Close your eyes for a moment and you can step into the past and recall a cherished way of life that has long since vanished.

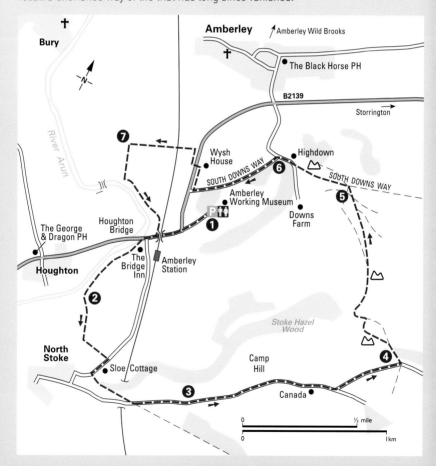

Route Directions

1 Turn left out of the car park and pass underneath the railway bridge. Begin to cross the road bridge spanning the Arun and then bear left at the footpath sign to reach a stile by a galvanised gate. After crossing a bridge and another stile, bear right on a riverside bank to the next stile and a few paces beyond it you reach a sluice. Bear left here.

2 Follow the path between trees, turn right on reaching a lane and pass Sloe Cottage. Turn left through a gate just beyond a caravan site to join a bridleway. Follow the path as it runs above the camping ground and emerge on a track by a bridleway sign. Cross the track here and join a rough lane, turning left.

3 The lane climbs gradually; the Arun can be seen below. Pass farm outbuildings and keep ahead, the lane dwindling to a track along this stretch. Veer left at the fork and follow the waymarked public right of way. Head for a signposted crossroads and turn left on a bridleway with a fence on your right.

4 Walk down the chalk track, pass through a gate and continue the steep descent. Look for two gates down below, set some distance apart. Cross to the right-hand gate and a reassuring bridleway sign is seen here. Follow the bridleway as it bends left, climbing steeply towards Downs Farm. Keep a fence on the left and follow the bridleway as it merges with a wide track.

5 Keep left at the next junction and follow the South Downs Way towards the entrance to Downs Farm. Fork right at the junction, signposted 'South Downs Way' and join a narrow footpath, which begins a steep descent. Drop down the slope until you reach a tarmac lane then turn right. On the right-hand side is a prominent house called Highdown.

6 Fork left on a lane (signposted 'The South Downs Way'). The attractions of Amberley Working Museum can be spotted down to the left. Immediately before the road junction, turn right and follow the South Downs Way parallel to the road. Cross the main road, continue on the other side and turn left on a concrete track over the railway line.

7 The track turns left here in front of a metal gate and continues to the bank of the River Arun. Swing left, veering slightly away from the river bank, to join a drive and then turn left at the road. Bear right to return to Amberley Working Museum and its car park.

Route facts

DISTANCE/TIME 7 miles (11.3km) 2h

MAP OS Explorer 121 Arundel & Pulborough

START Amberley Working Museum car park, by Amberley Station. Visit the museum, then leave your car here while on the walk, by kind permission of the museum management; grid ref: TQ 472332

TRACKS Riverside paths, downland tracks and some roads, 2 stiles.

GETTING TO THE START Amberley Working Museum is signed off the B2139, between Arundel and Storrington. Note that the car park is not available on days when special events are taking place at the museum, and also that it is locked at around 6pm.

THE PUB The Bridge Inn, Houghton Bridge. Tel: 01798 831619

❶ Short section beside and crossing busy road; suitable for children of all ages.

■ Visit

GOODWOOD AND THE TRUNDLE

Two prominent features of the Downs near West Dean are The Trundle and Goodwood Estate. Though marred by two ugly masts, The Trundle is a very special place on the South Downs. Enclosed by substantial Iron Age ramparts that define an ancient hill-fort, it has a grand view down to a huge section of coast from the Isle of Wight to the Seven Sisters. Inland, you can see the nearby racecourse at Goodwood, the estate that also encompasses a motor-racing circuit and the Cass Sculpture Foundation, with more than 70 commissioned sculptures in a beautiful setting within the grounds. Goodwood House, home of the Earl and Countess of March, is an elegant Regency mansion with paintings by Stubbs and Canaletto and magnificent French Sèvres porcelain.

PULBOROUGH BROOKS

MAP REF TQ0516

Come armed with binoculars for a day's birding at this important RSPB reserve, where geese, ducks and swans are drawn to the water, and hedgerow species proliferate too. From the visitor centre a marked trail leads past a viewpoint over the water meadows, which are often flooded in winter. Check the website for guided walks, family activities and beginners' courses. The visitor centre makes a handy lunch stop.

UPPARK MAP REF SU7817

On a hilltop site and the first great house in England to be built without an on-site water supply, Uppark found its geography worked against it in 1989 when the roof caught fire. The wind fanned the flames and water had to be pumped from more than 1 mile (1.6km) away. Over the six-year restoration (originally expected to take ten years) builders and craftspeople rediscovered long-lost skills and revived old traditions – such as recording the events of the day on chimney pots. The National Trust decided to re-create Uppark as it had been the day before the fire, a seamless join, complete with all the marks of age.

The house itself is built of brick in a Dutch style, and was designed in about 1690 by William Talman. It seems to sit high up on a plateau and is surrounded by landscaped pasture. Children can play ball games on the pleasant South Lawn. Inside, thanks to an extraordinary family history, the restored interiors are almost unchanged since Sir Matthew Fetherstonhaugh and his wife furnished it so lavishly on their honeymoon Grand Tour of Europe in the mid-18th century. Their son, Sir Harry, aged 71, married his 20-year old dairymaid Mary Ann in 1825 and died 21 years later. Mary Ann lived on with her sister, keeping things as they had been in Sir Harry's heyday: the Victorian age scarcely touched the house. By the 1900s the next owners had already started work on conserving the fragile textiles, and Uppark passed into the care of the National Trust in 1954.

The reconstructions are completely convincing; only a look at the folders of photographs in each room will show you where the joins are. Many stewards can relate personal stories of the day of the fire, such as the ceiling that collapsed minutes after the Prince Regent's bed was rescued. The basement of spacious kitchens and servants' quarters, which was abandoned in the 1900s, escaped with least damage and seems stranded in time, home to colonies of shrews and bats; the butler's room has a fold-down bed and a water gauge to show when the rooftop tanks need topping up. Also in the basement is the gigantic Uppark Doll's House, complete with Georgian furniture, glass and silverware. The stable block is rather more elaborate than the servants' dining hall, and the dairy outside is positively elegant.

WEST DEAN MAP REF SU8613

Nothing like a conventional museum, the Weald and Downland Open-Air Museum is more like a spread-out village consisting of relocated historic buildings rescued from town centre redevelopment, road and reservoir schemes in Sussex, Kent and Surrey – complete with watermill, ploughed fields and farm animals. It aims to promote public awareness and interest in old buildings and their surroundings, and does this brilliantly. There's something for everyone, from children who will be fascinated by the low doorways and open fires to the professional builder or craftsperson. The buildings look as though they have always been there. Most look as they would have been when first built, perhaps as medieval halls, with reproduction furnishings and usually a steward on hand to answer questions. There's a village school from 1895, a carpenter's shop and even an animal pound rescued from the route of the M25. Up in the woods, the pod-like modern gridshell building shows timber framing at its most innovative, and there are tours of the collection of building parts and rural tools kept in store underneath. Special events such as the Heavy Horse Spectacular and Working Animals Show (June) and Rare Breeds Show (July) are popular and there are demonstrations of flour milling and medieval cooking most days.

The open-air museum is part of the West Dean estate: you can glimpse the battlemented flint mansion (now West Dean College) beyond the medieval-style strip fields. Once a playground of King Edward VII and his entourage, West Dean Gardens run along one side of the seasonal stream of the River Lavant, with walks across downland pasture leading up to an arboretum. The rustic bridges and summer houses of the Spring Garden are Regency style, while the great pergola with vines, clematis, climbing hydrangea and roses, and the immense walled kitchen garden and glasshouses are from West Dean's Edwardian heyday.

■ Visit

STANSTED HOUSE

South of Uppark, this country house stands at the eastern end of a great grassy strip between the woodlands of Stansted Forest. The strip was created as a vista for the house, and as a public footpath runs for most of its length you can enjoy a walk from Rowland's Castle to the house. Like Uppark, Stansted House burned down and was faithfully rebuilt: the fire was in 1900, and its atmosphere today is very much that of an Edwardian mansion. It contains the family possessions of the Earls of Bessborough, its last owners.

■ TOURIST INFORMATION CENTRES

Arundel
61 High Street.
Tel: 01903 882268

Bognor Regis
Belmont Street.
Tel: 01243 823140

Chichester
29a South Street.
Tel: 01243 775888 or
01243 539435
www.visitchichester.org

Littlehampton
Look & Sea! Centre
63–65 Surrey Street.
Tel: 01903 721866

Midhurst
North Street.
Tel: 01730 817322

Petworth
The Old Bakery.
Tel: 01798 343523

■ PLACES OF INTEREST

Amberley Working Museum
Tel: 01798 831370;
www.amberleymuseum.co.uk

Arundel Castle
Tel: 01903 882173;
www.arundelcastle.org.uk

Arundel History Store
Mill Road car park.
Tel: 01903 885708;
www.arundelmuseum.org.uk

Arundel Wetland Centre
Mill Road, Arundel.
Tel: 01903 883355;
www.wwt.org.uk

Bignor Roman Villa
Bignor. Tel: 01798 869259

Cass Sculpture Foundation
Goodwood.
Tel: 01243 538449;
www.sculpture.org.uk

Earnley Butterflies and Gardens
133 Almodington Lane,
Earnley, nr Chichester.
Tel: 01243 512637

Fishbourne Roman Palace
Fishbourne, Chichester.
Tel: 01243 785859;
www.sussexpast.co.uk

Look & Sea! Centre
63–65 Surrey Street,
Littlehampton.
Tel: 01903 718984;
www.lookandsea.co.uk

Nutbourne Vineyard Trail
Pulborough.
Tel: 01798 815196;
www.nutbournevineyards.com

Pallant House Gallery
Chichester.
Tel: 01243 774557;
www.pallant.org.uk

Petworth House & Park
Petworth.
Tel: 01798 343929; www.
nationaltrust.org.uk/petworth

Pulborough Brooks Nature Reserve
Tel: 01798 875851;
www.rspb.org.uk

South Downs Planetarium
Sir Patrick Moore Building,
Kingsham Farm,
Kingsham Road,
Chichester.
Tel: 01243 774400;
www.southdowns.org.uk

Stansted House
Stansted Park,
Rowlands Castle.
Tel: 023 9241 2265;
www.stanstedpark.co.uk

Tangmere Military Aviation Museum
Tel: 01243 790090; www.
tangmere-museum.org.uk

Uppark House & Garden
South Harting.
Tel: 01730 825827; www.
nationaltrust.org.uk/uppark

Weald & Downland Open-Air Museum
Singleton.
Tel: 01243 811348;
www.wealddown.co.uk

West Dean Gardens
West Dean.
Tel: 01243 811301;
www.westdean.org.uk

■ FOR CHILDREN

Arundel Ghost Experience
Old Town Hall,
Duke's Path Entrance,
High Street.
Tel: 01903 889821

Fishers Farm Park
Wisborough Green,
near Billingshurst.
Tel: 01403 700063;
www.fishersfarmpark.co.uk

Harbour Park
Littlehampton.
Tel: 01903 721200;
www.harbourpark.com
Play fantasy golf, pan for
gold, ride the water chute and
encounter the Horror Hotel!

■ SHOPPING

ARUNDEL

Pallant of Arundel
The Square.
Tel: 01903 882288;
www.pallantofarundel.co.uk
A chic delicatessen.

Peglers Expedition Advisers and Suppliers
69 Tarrant Street.
Tel: 01903 883375;
www.peglers.co.uk
Four shops in the town.

The Walking Stick Shop
Old Print Works.
Tel: 01903 883796;
www.walkingstickshop.co.uk

CHICHESTER
High street and independent
shops, all within strolling
distance of the cathedral.

J & G Gallery
28 West Street.
Tel: 01243 788828;
www.jggallery.co.uk

Montezuma's
29 East Street.
Tel: 01243 537385;
www.montezumas.co.uk
Handmade chocolates.

Timothy Roe
12 South Street.
Tel: 01243 538313;
www.timothyroe.com
Hand-crafted jewellery.

MIDHURST

Harvey's Bottle and Jug
Red Lion Street.
Tel: 01730 810709;
www.harveys.org.uk
Local Harvey's beers.

■ LOCAL SPECIALITIES

Adsdean Farm Shop
Funtington, Chichester.
Tel: 01243 575212;
www.adsdeanfarm.co.uk

Farmers' Markets
Arundel, 3rd Sat.
Chichester, 1st and 3rd Fri.
Midhurst, 4th Sat.
Petworth, 4th Sat.

■ PERFORMING ARTS

Chichester Festival Theatre
Oaklands Park.
Tel: 01243 784437;
www.cft.org.uk

■ OUTDOOR ACTIVITIES

BOAT TRIPS

Arundel Boatyard
Mill Road, Arundel.
Tel: 01903 882609;
www.riveraruncruises.com

Chichester Harbour Water Tours
Tel: 01243 670504;
www.chichesterharbour
watertours.co.uk

Solar Heritage Boat Tours
Itchenor.
Tel: 01243 513275;
www.conservancy.co.uk

HORSE-RACING

Fontwell Park Racecourse
Arundel.
Tel: 01243 543335;
www.fontwellpark.co.uk

Goodwood Race Course
Tel: 01243 755022;
www.goodwood.co.uk

MOTOR RACING

Goodwood Circuit
Tel: 01243 755055;
www.goodwood.co.uk

WATER SPORTS

Chichester Watersports
Coach Road, Chichester.
Tel: 01243 776439; www.
chichesterwatersports.co.uk

■ ANNUAL EVENTS & CUSTOMS

Arundel
Corpus Christi,
May–Jun, 60 days after
Easter, in the Cathedral.
Tel: 01903 882297
Arundel Festival,
late Aug–early Sep;
www.arundelfestival.co.uk

Chichester
Chichester Festivities,
Jul. Tel: 01243 528356;
www.chifest.org.uk

Goodwood
Festival of Speed,
early Jul. Tel: 01243 755000;
www.goodwood.co.uk.
Goodwood Revival, Sep.

Littlehampton
Seafront Festival,
end Jul.

Petworth
Petworth Festival,
Jul–Aug.
Tel: 01798 344576;
www.petworthfestival.org.uk

CHICHESTER & ARUNDEL

Tea Rooms

Belindas Tea Room
13 Tarrant Street, Arundel BN18 9DG. Tel: 01903 882977

A white-painted cottage in characterful Tarrant Street. Go down the steps to an old English interior, with copper and brassware on the walls. Belindas serves cream teas, sandwiches and jacket potatoes, with a tempting list of traditional desserts.

Cathedral Cloisters Café
Chichester Cathedral, Chichester PO19 1PX Tel: 01243 782595

Walk into the cathedral cloisters and you'll find this splendid self-service café. Airy and modern in style, it offers a range of afternoon teas and daily specials, as well as Sunday lunch. There is a large walled garden.

Comestibles
Delicatessen and Café
Red Lion Street, Midhurst GU29 9PB. Tel: 01730 813400

Opposite the Harvey's Bottle and Jug shop in the prettiest part of town, Comestibles serves a range of jacket potatoes, sandwiches, breakfasts and salads. Its deli has locally produced treats such as organic chocolate, as well as olive oils, preserves and biscuits.

Tiffins of Petworth
1 Leppards, High Street, Petworth GU28 0AU Tel: 01798 344560

Tea rooms and restaurant with pastel-painted wooden tables and chairs, and words of wisdom on the walls. Tiffins serves breakfasts and lunches with the likes of lasagne and fisherman's pie alongside teas, coffees and home-made cakes. It also displays and sells a whole menagerie of ceramic and porcelain animals and other gifts and knick-knacks.

Pubs

The Fox Goes Free
Charlton PO18 0HU Tel: 01243 811461

A perfect village pub, with a snug, dark old-fashioned interior and a spacious garden (lit up in the evening) shaded by apple trees and looking out to the South Downs. The menu changes frequently and ingredients are carefully chosen.

George and Dragon
Burpham BN18 9RR Tel: 01903 883131

Not far from Arundel and on the east bank of the River Arun, the village of Burpham (pronounced Burfam) is a choice spot for strolls along the river and on to the Downs,

so this dining pub makes a rewarding objective, with lunchtime and evening bar food and four real ales. The restaurant upstairs has views of the South Downs, while the garden looks across the valley. Do book ahead to be sure of a table.

The Star and Garter
East Dean GU29 0JY Tel: 01243 811318

Handy for the Weald and Downland Museum, this is a dining pub located in a lovely downland village. It's roomy and furnished in the country style, with a successful mix of both antique and modern furnishings. The bar menu features seafood and includes standard ploughman's. The terrace has parasols and heaters, and there's a lawn with picnic tables.

The Three Horseshoes
Elsted, BU29 0JY Tel: 01730 825746

Just what a country pub should be – with latched doors, worn tiled floors, high-back settles, a miscellany of old furniture and a vast inglenook fireplace. The garden is an enticing place to linger on a summer's day. Bar food includes soup, tasty ploughman's, hearty specials and sumptuous puddings.

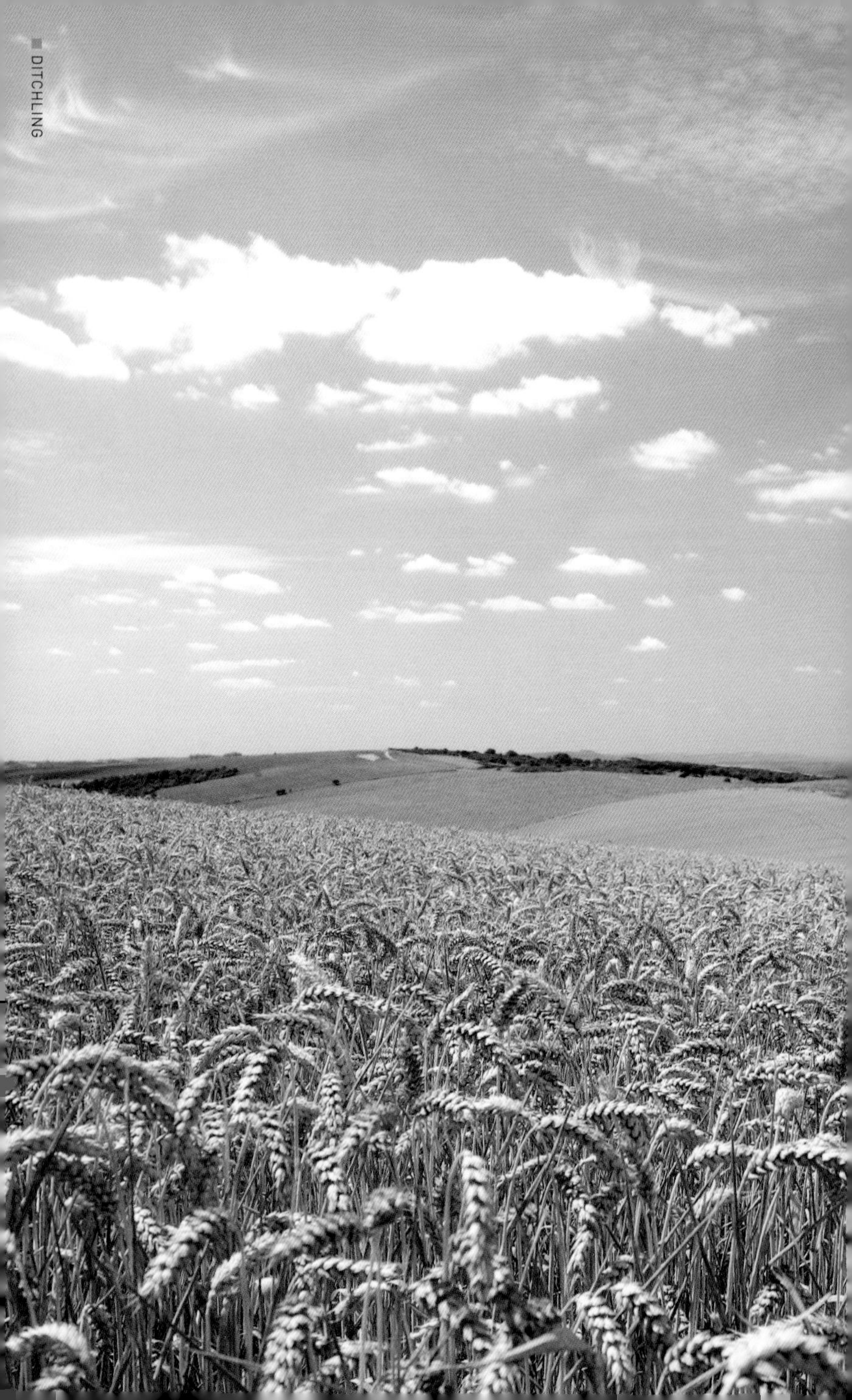

Brighton & Around

Exuberant, quirky and even outrageous, Brighton is one of the liveliest coastal towns in Britain with traditional seaside fun alongside masses for those into sea and surf, clubbing, performing arts, gay culture or just watching the crowds go by. The exotic Royal Pavilion forms the centrepiece of some superb Regency architecture. Cissbury Ring, Ditchling Beacon and Devil's Dyke are favourite fresh-air fixes on the South Downs, while further north, Nymans is a lusciously colour-laden garden.

7 Walk start point   **1** Cycle start point

DITCHLING

Unmissable attractions

Go Regency in the riot of colour that is Brighton Pavilion...see a sofa shaped like Mae West's lips at Brighton Museum and Art Gallery...shop for vintage clothes and retro gifts in Brighton's funky North Laine...head for Brighton's bracing seafront and take your chances on the West Pier amusements, have your palm read or your hair braided, or just sit and watch the world go by from the comfort of a beach bar...take a bus up to Devil's Dyke and stroll along the South Downs Way...visit Nymans Garden in early summer to see the dazzling display of rhododendrons and azaleas...marvel at the inventiveness of Shoreham's houseboat dwellers and go on to watch the light aircraft from the café at the art deco airport.

1 Devil's Dyke
The Devil's Dyke consists of 183 acres (74ha) of beautiful open downland which is dotted with orchids and cowslips in spring and early summer. It lies within the South Downs National Park.

2 Brighton
A traditional carousel on the seafront at Brighton complements the attractions found on Brighton Pier.

3 South Downs Way
A signpost directs people to the South Downs Way, a national trail for walkers, cyclists and horse-riders, between the city of Winchester and the seaside town of Eastbourne. It has some of its best moments near Brighton.

4 Ditchling
The quiet roads and lanes around the picturesque village of Ditchling pass through glorious downland countryside.

BRIGHTON & HOVE

MAP REF TQ3005

Brighton is unmistakably cosmopolitan, fun-loving and sophisticated, and the long-standing weekend playground for Londoners as the nearest and most happening southern seaside town. The cliché that it's a place for romantic frolics has been overtaken by its newer image as a gay capital, an arty vibrant place that keeps going until the small hours. The presence of some 50,000 students from the Brighton and Sussex university campuses at nearby Falmer, in addition to many language schools, compounds the youthful feel.

The city divides into its own distinct 'villages'. However, the border between Brighton and Hove is bewildering, and not even the locals necessarily know whether a certain street is in Brighton or 'Hove actually' – as it's jovially known.

It was the Prince Regent's first visits in 1783 that really put Brighton at the height of fashion. This was the place to see and be seen: the elegant squares, terraces and crescents attest to this time, and the Royal Pavilion became the most spectacular architectural flight of fancy Britain has ever witnessed.

The beachfront changes in character from one moment to the next. Ornate Victorian lamp posts, aqua-coloured railings and the creamy white stucco frontages characterise one of the finest seaside townscapes in Britain, with many elegant bow-windowed Regency and grand Victorian façades, stretching from Brunswick Square and Adelaide Crescent in Hove to the west, to Kemp Town in the east. At the middle of it all, ornate Brighton Pier has a funfair with some white-knuckle rides. Near its entrance, the Brighton Sea Life Centre has displays including a walk-through glass tunnel, where giant turtles and sharks float above your head to give a spectacular view of the underwater world. Time your visit to coincide with the daily shark and turtle feeds.

From here you can ride the Volks Electric Railway, opened 1883, where quaintly miniature carriages trundle the 1.5 miles (2.4km) to Black Rock station. Close to Black Rock are the terraces and crescents that make up Lewes Crescent in Kemp Town, Brighton's grandest Regency seafront buildings.

To the east, Brighton Marina is a huge modern complex with outlet shopping, bowling, an eight-screen cinema, prestigious apartment complexes and waterfront restaurants and cafés. It's all very new world, and among all this the endearing scruffiness of the fishing fleet looks somewhat out of place. From here you can walk on the seafront promenade beneath the chalk cliffs, passing close by Roedean girls' boarding school and residential Saltdean with its restored art deco lido. The path ends at Rottingdean which has attractive public gardens, a tea room and a museum devoted to its former resident Rudyard Kipling.

West of Brighton Pier is the liveliest part of the beachfront. The booths under the esplanade are home to an artistic quarter, with little galleries alongside palmists, cockles and jellied eel stalls, bucket and spade shops, bars, henna tattooists and hair-braiders. Look out for the tiny Mechanical Memories Museum, where you can buy big old pennies to operate vintage machines and see what the butler saw (not much), or activate an animated jazz band. There's also an 1888 carousel and an absorbing little Fishing Museum, chronicling Brighton's association with its original livelihood.

At night, the action revolves around the beachfront clubs, plus there are free performances at the Ellipse area, open-air cinema and music on the beach. The Brighton Centre has shows and gigs, with many big-name bands. By the beach near the ornate bandstand (under restoration) is a free paddling pool and playground. Major plans are afoot to transform the seafront. The future may see the erection of the i360 viewing tower. This would be by the skeletal ruin of the West Pier, kept as a landmark, and as a winter roosting point for tens of thousands of starlings which take off in a spectacular billowing cloud at dusk.

Just behind the seafront from the west side of the Brighton Pier is The Lanes, an intricate knot of little streets and alleys based on the old fishing port of Brighthelmstone. It's now packed with restaurants, boutiques, and jewellery and clothes shops, with tempting cooking smells periodically wafting from doorways. A couple of oyster bars recall Brighton's days as a Victorian resort, and here and there you can find traces of flint-fronted fishermen's cottages.

Between the railway station and the Royal Pavilion is the North Laine – radically different from The Lanes. Here a series of small streets (Sydney Street, Kensington Street, Gardner Street and Bond Street) have evolved into a very alternative shopping and promenading area, with funky, sometimes outrageous shop fronts and selling products such as crystals, various body piercings, religious artefacts, bonsai trees, vintage clothes and ethnic furniture. Pavement cafés, delis and market stalls abound, but it quietens down in the evening. Away from the shops are cottagey little residential streets, and just north in Ann Street is St Bartholomew's (completed 1874), the most visually extraordinary of Brighton's churches – barn-like from the outside but revealing a rich interior with a gold mosaic and mother-of-pearl ceiling and a Byzantine-style baldachin. To find the North Laine from the station, start with your back to the station, bear slightly right then turn immediately left downhill right underneath the station on Trafalgar Street, passing the Brighton Toy and Model Museum, a nostalgia-fest of thousands of toys, model railway layouts, dolls, Meccano and puppets.

■ Visit

PRESTON MANOR

Life for the gentry and their servants in Edwardian times is perfectly evoked at this former country house, now engulfed in the northern suburb of Preston Park.

Ticking clocks and the smell of polished furniture greet you in the opulent entrance hall and main living rooms, and there are pictures, furniture and all sorts of assorted family belongings, including a child's nursery and a Heath Robinson-like 'Aspirator' vacuum cleaner. On the stairs, three views of the house in the 19th century show it in its original downland setting. The kitchen and servants hall give glimpses of life 'below stairs'.

At 80 Trafalgar Street is O Contemporary, Brighton's biggest commercial art gallery, with all works for sale. Artists have included Andy Warhol, Damien Hirst, Tracey Emin and David Hockney.

Just inland from The Lanes is the heart of Regency Brighton and the astonishing Royal Pavilion. Originally a simple farmhouse, it became a classical 'Marine Pavilion' before John Nash transformed it between 1815 and 1823 for the Prince Regent, later George IV, into an Indian fantasy of domes and minarets. George came here to his

Visit

DEVIL'S DYKE
Another popular place to enjoy the view or fly a kite from the top of the Downs is further west of Ditchling Beacon at Devil's Dyke, which you can reach by bus from Brighton (open-topped bus no. 77 from the seafront or rail station, or no. 79 from the rail station). Not everyone finds the Devil's Dyke itself – an impressively deep dry valley just behind the Devil's Dyke Hotel.

Visit

NYMANS GARDEN
Another delectably romantic garden that is ablaze with colour in early summer, Nymans was created in the 20th century by three generations of the Messel family and is now owned by the National Trust. Some 30 acres (12ha) of gardens are laid out around the mansion in a way that guarantees a surprise vista at every turn. There are changes in level and mood, with statuary, a stone loggia, a sunken lawn, a pergola, a heather garden and much more besides. The trees are magnificent, and beyond this you can wander the woodland paths through the surrounding estate.

seaside palace for arts, racing and endless partying: he relished being right in the centre of things. You can wander through one of the two Indian-style outer gates either side of the restored gardens, which are a delightful green oasis, and stop to admire the building's engaging eccentricity from outside, but it gives no hint of the riot of extravagant chinoiserie. Beyond the Long Gallery, lit by painted glass ceiling lights and with a cast-iron 'bamboo' staircase, is the magnificent Banqueting Room, where a gilded dragon holds an exotic chandelier beneath the domed ceiling. The lavish detailing extends to the kitchens, where cast-iron columns topped with painted copper palm leaves bear the high ceiling. Upstairs the Queen Adelaide tea rooms make an unrivalled sitting place overlooking the gardens. Across the Pavilion Gardens and housed within the former Pavilion stables and riding school, the Brighton Museum and Art Gallery is one of Brighton's best free sights. There's something for everyone here – fashion, paintings, the story of Brighton's growth and change, art nouveau furniture, a Discovery Gallery for children and a fascinating display entitled Mr Willett's Popular Pottery – a unique collection of ceramics depicting British social history over three centuries. The café up on the balcony over the main hall is excellent.

Near Brighton's Victorian clock tower, Churchill Square, Brighton's covered shopping centre, boasts more than 80 stores under one roof. From there, Western Road has other names such as Marks and Spencer, though the scale soon gets smaller. There are delightful hilly streets just to the north, rising up to the Montpellier area – some of Brighton and Hove's most eye-catching Regency villas and terraces, and there's more of the same along the seafront into the Brunswick area. Preston Street has a concentration of ethnic restaurants.

Further west into Hove, St Andrews Church, in Waterloo Street, is a striking Regency Italian Renaissance style Grade I listed church, designed in 1827 by Sir Charles Barry. In the middle of Victorian Hove is the enjoyably eclectic Hove Museum & Art Gallery with an interactive toy gallery done out as a wizard's attic, paintings and local history. The highlight is the film gallery showing the work of Hove film-makers Smith and Williamson from around 1900. It's engaging stuff: touching little moral tales about people ending up in workhouses. Outside, the grand Jaipur Gate was made for the Colonial and Indian Exhibition of 1886.

CISSBURY RING MAP REF TQ1408

A dead-end road leads up from Findon on to the Downs beneath the striking ancient site of Cissbury Ring. From the car park, it takes a few minutes to walk up to the ramparts of this formidable hill-fort dating from about 350 BC. From here the view takes in the coast, from Beachy Head to the Isle of Wight. The ramparts would have been built up with a timber stockade, and the enclosed area within would have had a sizeable community, living in thatched round houses, with areas for cooking, weaving, spinning and knapping flints, as well as pits for storing food.

Turn right along the ramparts and you'll shortly find a hummocky, bushy area that is much older than the fort: this is one of only ten known neolithic flint mines in England. Here, between about 4500 BC and 2300 BC, some of the earliest farming communities used picks made of antlers to mine for flint: the shafts have been filled in, but have sunk in the middle and appear as pits.

CLAYTON MAP REF TQ3013

This tiny village, stretched along narrow Underhill Lane and snug beneath the Downs, harbours some notable curios. Here the London to Brighton railway enters a tunnel through a spectacular castle-like portal, with arrow-slits and battlemented turrets, and which can be glimpsed from the road. In the village itself, St John's Church has an extraordinary interior, embellished by rare pre-Norman wall paintings which have survived the centuries remarkably well; depictions include the *Last Judgement*, *Christ in Glory* and the *Fall of Satan*. High up on the downs above the village are two Clayton Windmills known as Jack and Jill: 'Jill' is a postmill in working order and open most summer Sunday and Bank Holiday afternoons, while 'Jack', a private house, is a tower mill. Windmills were once a common feature of the South Downs, but this is the only place where two still stand side by side. You can walk along the South Downs Way to Ditchling Beacon from here, while to the west rises Wolstonbury Hill, an outlier of the downs, designated a Site of Special Scientific Interest for its rare chalk-loving flora.

A Circuit of Devil's Dyke by Poynings

This is a fine walk with glimpses over the most famous of all the dry chalk valleys. Devil's Dyke is a geological quirk – a spectacular, steep-sided downland combe or cleft 300ft (91m) deep and half a mile (800m) long. It was probably cut by glacial meltwaters millions of years ago in the ice age. Rising to over 600ft (183m), views from this beauty spot stretch for miles in all directions. The artist John Constable described this view as the grandest in the world, which is fine praise indeed. In good weather the slopes can be busy with people, while in the skies hang-gliders swoop over the grassy downland. However, away from the car park and chalk slopes the walk heads for more peaceful surroundings.

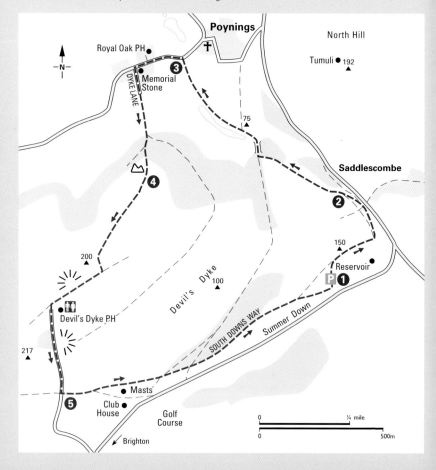

Route Directions

1 From the Summer Down car park go through the kissing gate and then veer right. Join the South Downs Way and follow it alongside lines of trees. Soon the path curves left and drops down to the road. Part company with the South Downs Way at this point, as it crosses over to join the private road to Saddlescombe Farm, and follow the verge for about 75yds (69m). Bear left at the footpath sign and drop down the bank to a stile.

2 Follow the line of the tarmac lane as it curves right to reach a waymark. Leave the lane and walk ahead alongside power lines, keeping the line of trees and bushes on the right. Look for a narrow path disappearing into the vegetation and make for a stile. Drop down some steps into the woods and turn right at a junction with a bridleway. Take the path running off half left and follow it between fields and a wooded dell. Pass over a stile and continue to a stile in the left boundary. Cross a footbridge to a further stile and now turn right towards Poynings.

3 Head for a gate and footpath sign and turn left at the road.

Follow the parallel path along to the Royal Oak and then continue to Dyke Lane on the left. There is a memorial stone here, dedicated to the memory of George Stephen Cave Cuttress, a resident of Poynings for over 50 years, and erected by his widow. Follow the tarmac bridleway and soon it narrows to a path. On reaching the fork, by a National Trust sign for Devil's Dyke, veer right and begin climbing the steps.

4 Follow the path up to a gate and continue up the stairs. From the higher ground there are breathtaking views to the north and west. Make for a kissing gate and head up the slope towards the inn. Keep the Devil's Dyke pub on your left and take the road round to the left, passing a bridleway on the left. Follow the path parallel to the road and look to the left for a definitive view of Devil's Dyke.

5 Head for the South Downs Way and turn left by a National Trust sign for Summer Down to a stile and gate. Follow the trail, keeping Devil's Dyke down to your left, and eventually you reach a stile leading into Summer Down car park where you started this walk.

Route facts

DISTANCE/TIME 2.75 miles (4.4km) 1h30

MAP OS Explorer 122 South Downs Way: Steyning to Newhaven

START Free car park, Summer Down; grid ref: TQ 269112

TRACKS Field and woodland paths, 7 stiles.

GETTING TO THE START Poynings is north of Brighton, west of the A23. Take the A281 for Henfield, then turn left for Poynings. Turn left in front of the church, then at the next T-junction, turn right. Follow this road for about 1 mile (1.6km) and turn right, signposted 'Dyke'. The car park is on the right after about 500yds (457m).

THE PUB Royal Oak, Poynings. Tel: 01273 857389; www.royaloakpoynings.biz

❶ Steep steps up the South Downs. Suitable for fitter, older children.

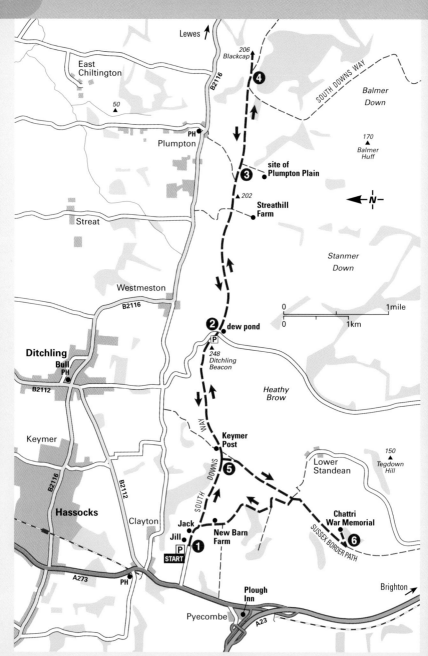

Lewes

East
Chiltington

206
Blackcap

④

SOUTH DOWNS WAY

Balmer
Down

B2116

50

170
Balmer
Huff

PH
Plumpton

③

site of
Plumpton Plain

202

Streathill
Farm

N

Street

Stanmer
Down

Westmeston

B2116

0   1mile
0   1km

② dew pond

P

248
Ditchling
Beacon

Ditchling

Bull
PH

B2112

Heathy
Brow

Keymer

B2116

B2112

WAY

Keymer
Post

⑤

Lower
Standean

150
Tegdown
Hill

Hassocks

SOUTH DOWNS

Clayton

Jack

New Barn
Farm

Chattri
War Memorial

⑥

Jill

P

START

①

SUSSEX BORDER PATH

A273

PH

Plough
Inn

Brighton

Pyecombe

A23

Ditchling Beacon and the Chattri War Memorial

Cycle along one of the most spectacular sections of the South Downs, with views all the way. The route passes two windmills called Jack (now a private house) and Jill, and the Chattri War Memorial, dedicated to Indian servicemen who lost their lives in the First World War.

Route Directions

1 Turn left out of the car park, signposted 'public bridleway to Ditchling Beacon', ignore a driveway, left, to Jack Windmill and another left track. Fork left uphill at a junction, signposted 'South Downs Way'. Blue arrow markers with acorn motifs denote the South Downs Way, which you follow for most of the ride. The stony track rises steeply at first, but it soon levels out.

2 From Ditchling Beacon car park cross the road and take the South Downs Way opposite. The route climbs up two grassy rises and drops to cross a narrow farm road. Here the clay surface can be sticky after rain.

3 After the next left, a descending fork (which you avoid), look for a track on the right, marked with a blue arrow which leads to the site of Plumpton Plain, a Bronze Age settlement. Carry on along the South Downs Way.

4 Beyond a gate is a National Trust sign for Blackcap. Walk up to the summit by forking left to the trig point.

5 Unless you want to return along the South Downs Way, turn left at the top of the main ascent after Ditchling Beacon (where Jack Windmill comes into view). It's marked with a blue arrow and a sign 'Chattri and the windmills' (just after another junction by a signpost on the right marked 'Keymer Post'. Descend with Brighton in view ahead, at the second gate (waymarked 'Chattri and the windmills' no. 13), detour to the Chattri war memorial.

6 After the next gate, leave your bike and walk down to the war memorial. Return to the junction at the previous gate, turn left, following signs: the route bends right (no. 44) on a fenced path, left (no. 45), then downhill and turns right leaving the indicated route 'Chattri and

Route facts

DISTANCE/TIME 11 miles (17.7km) 3h

MAP OS Explorer 122 South Downs Way: Steyning to Newhaven

START Free car park by Jack and Jill windmills; grid ref: TQ 304134. Alternative start: Ditchling Beacon car park, south of Ditchling; grid ref: TQ 333131

TRACKS: Quite bumpy chalk and grass tracks, with some sections along clay.

GETTING TO THE START Jack and Jill windmills: follow the A273 south from Hassocks, turn left just before Pyecombe up Mill Lane. Ditchling Beacon: follow the B2112 south, fork left on the road leading up to Ditchling Beacon and its car park (begin at Point 2).

CYCLE HIRE M's Cycle Hire 07852 986165; www.m-cyclehire.co.uk. Will deliver and pick up bikes free anywhere between Chichester and Lewes.

THE PUB The Bull, Ditchling. Tel: 01273 843147

❶ An energetic ride, with several ascents and descents – not suitable for young children.

the windmills' (at no. 46), which continues ahead. The track crosses the South Downs Way through a farm to the Jack and Jill windmills and the car park.

DITCHLING MAP REF TQ3315

The photogenic old village of Ditchling looks out to one of the choicest, most-frequented parts of the South Downs. The Bull pub and a couple of tea rooms make good stopping points in the village, and in a former Victorian school near the church the Ditchling Museum has a local collection and changing exhibitions. It also remembers the work of pioneer calligraphers Eric Gill and Edward Johnston (who devised the distinctive sans serif script used by London Transport).

Gill came here with his apprentice in 1907, and soon a community of craftsmen and artists was established, who adhered to principles of the Arts and Crafts Movement; they set up workshops and a chapel, and the community continued until 1989, after which the complex was demolished.

From the village, a road climbs up to Ditchling Beacon, at 813 feet (248m) the highest point on the South Downs. It's a great place to come to for a picnic, fly a kite, paraglide (or watch), walk a stretch of the South Downs Way, or just drink in the big view over the Weald and across to the high ridge of greensand hills that include the prominent escarpment of Black Down, the highest point in Sussex at 919 feet (280m).

The landscape hereabouts contains all sorts of evidence of prehistoric settlers, including burial mounds and ancient systems, and a stroll eastwards along the top of the escarpment leads close to the site of a Bronze Age settlement at Plumpton Plain.

SHOREHAM-BY-SEA

MAP REF TQ2205

An art deco airport, house boats and medieval heritage make up an unlikely list of attractions here: the town is not really on the mainstream tourist map, but has great curiosity value for those with a taste for the quirky and offbeat. Beyond conventional outskirts, you'll find the compact old centre of what is known as New Shoreham, still village-like with attractive old cottages fronted with beach pebbles, and the impressively preserved, largely Norman church, which has magnificent arches. Facing the yacht-filled Adur estuary not far away is the Marlipins Museum, which houses displays of local and maritime history in a 12th-century building.

■ Activity

WALK THE MONARCH'S WAY TO CHANCTONBURY RING

From Bramber Castle or the south end of Steyning, the Monarch's Way long-distance path leads up to join the South Downs Way and follow the escarpment for 2.5 miles (4km) to the clump of beech trees known as Chanctonbury Ring. This is one of the most striking features on the Downs, but it is less impressive than it was. Sadly the ferocious storm that swept through southeast England in October 1987 wrought great damage, and many of the trees here were felled in a few hours. You can make out Iron Age ramparts of a hill-fort enclosing the wooded site, within which is the site of a Romano-British temple – when the trees fell in 1987, more of the archaeology was revealed. For a short walk there's also a car park just below Chanctonbury Ring, off the A283 northwest of Steyning.

Walk over the footbridge across the harbour, and on the other side on the right you'll notice the houseboats that are part of one of Sussex's most distinctive communities. It grew up after 1945 to help remedy the housing shortage created by the disappearance of the ramshackle 'bungalow town' of converted railway carriages that existed near by. All manner of ancient craft, some about 100 years old, have been assembled one by one, and added to and adapted: they include a military torpedo boat, river barges, an oyster smack, a steam yacht, various gun boats and a mine sweeper. One former passenger ferry has been bizarrely embellished with a coach split lengthwise and added on either side, and many have tiny little gardens full of pot plants and snoozing cats. Although the boats themselves are private, you get an excellent view of them by walking along the waterfront path past their 'front doors'.

■ Visit

SHOREHAM AIRPORT

Shoreham Airport, the United Kingdom's oldest licensed airfield, really evokes the pioneering days of aviation, with its lovingly maintained Art Deco terminal building. All very different from the hectic world of Heathrow or Gatwick, this is a popular place for families to come and watch the comings and goings of the small aircraft, which still include some scheduled public flights to France. The café is good value and the visitor centre next door displays some mementoes. It's well signposted by road; or walk on past the houseboats along the river, cross a busy road and continue through meadows to reach the airport.

STEYNING MAP REF TQ1712

The silting-up of Steyning's riverside harbour in medieval times resulted in it being stranded as a small country town with a most impressive array of historic buildings. The best concentration is in Church Street where the overhanging timber-framed buildings and early brick façades date mostly from the 15th to the 17th centuries. Look out for the cottage inscribed 'This is Harry Gough's House, 1771', installed by the local MP asserting his rights over a problematic tenant. In a modern building beyond Church Street, near the library, is a well laid-out local history museum (free). The long High Street has independent food shops, pubs and cafés, and you can browse for gifts and homeware at Cobblestone Walk.

St Andrew's Church has a massive tower faced in neat chequerboard patterns of flint and stone, but almost dwarfed by the height of the nave with its second upper row of windows. The resemblance to a French abbey is no coincidence, since it was built by Norman monks from Fécamp between the late 11th and mid-12th centuries. The interior is just as impressive with huge dog-toothed Norman arches, carved capitals and an early font in Sussex marble supported by four slender pillars. Inside the church porch is a mysterious long stone marked with symbols, discovered in 1938 laid face down at the edge of the churchyard. The name Steyning could mean 'people of the stone', and it's possible that the stone is an ancient pagan idol, demoted when St Cuthman converted the area to Christianity around AD 750. There are many legends associated with the saint: a recent sculpture of him gazes pensively at the site of his church. It was re-dedicated in favour of St Andrew in 1260 by French monks who had little time for the Cuthman stories.

Almost joined to Steyning is the village of Bramber, with its long flower-hung main street spanning the river. The entrance to its much-battered castle is at the road junction with the A283. There's free access to the ruins; the impressive fragment of stonework is all that remains of the gatehouse tower.

WORTHING MAP REF TQ1503

A big, spreading seaside town that is effectively an extension of the Brighton and Hove conurbation, Worthing is as much a residential and retirement place as a resort, but it's a pleasant enough visit to come shopping (with a good range of high street shops) and wander the seafront with its fairy lights, flower beds, pier and palm trees. Liverpool Terrace and Montague Place preserve some good-looking early 19th-century frontages, and Montague Street forms part of the pleasant pedestrianised shopping area. In Chapel Road, the Worthing Museum and Art Gallery has an excellent archaeology section as well as collections of toys, decorative art, local history and costumes from times past.

By the shingle beach (sand at low tide), the pier was mostly rebuilt in the 1930s after a fire: it's in the distinctive International style, complete with art deco clock. The Pavilion Theatre at the shore end with its Parisian-looking entrance was part of an earlier pier.

■ Visit

SOMPTING CHURCH

Just outside the northern fringes of Worthing, and on the far side of the A27, Sompting church stands by itself. It's often regarded as Sussex's best example of a Saxon church, though you have to do a bit of detective work as most of it is later – the Saxon arch in the nave is one of the most visible early features; look also for a blocked door in the north wall – a 'devil's door' that would have been left open at a baptism to allow evil spirits to depart from a child's heart. For years the Saxon-style tower was thought to have been part of the original structure, but tree-ring dating of the timbers suggests that it is medieval.

Opposite, by the Dome Cinema, Macari's ice cream parlour is an institution in Worthing, advertising 24 flavours of home-made ice cream, and there's a collection of lively bars and restaurants.

At Goring Gap (between Ferring and Goring, west of Worthing) the coastal Marine Drive runs beside a wide strip of short grass ideal for games and picnics, with a shingle beach beyond, screened by a windswept bank of trees. Farmland stretches inland, giving an undeveloped view of the Downs. The only buildings are screened by the Ilex Avenue of 400 evergreen oaks, planted around 1840 as a carriage road for Goring Hall.

From the A27 just outside Worthing – or from the South Downs Way – you can see Lancing College, one of the area's leading public schools. The tall, spikily Gothic chapel (among English churches only Westminster Abbey, York Minster and Liverpool Anglican Cathedral are higher) is open to the public.

■ TOURIST INFORMATION CENTRES

Brighton
Royal Pavilion Shop.
Tel: 0906 711 2255;
www.visitbrighton.com

Burgess Hill
96 Church Walk.
Tel: 01444 238202

Worthing
Chapel Road.
Tel: 01903 221307

■ PLACES OF INTEREST

Brighton Museum & Art Gallery
Royal Pavilion Gardens.
Tel: 03000 290900; www.brighton-hove-rpml.org.uk

Ditchling Museum
Church Lane, Ditchling.
Tel: 01273 844744;
www.ditchling-museum.com

Leonardslee
Lower Beeding, Horsham.
Tel: 01403 891212;
www.leonardslee.com

Preston Manor
Preston Drove.
Tel: 03000 290900; www.brighton-hove-rpml.org.uk

Royal Pavilion
Church Street, Brighton.
Tel: 03000 290900; www.brighton-hove-rpml.org.uk

Steyning Museum
Church Street, Steyning.
Tel: 01903 813333;
www.steyningmuseum.org.uk

Worthing Museum & Art Gallery
Tel: 01903 221067 (Mon–Fri);
01903 221448 (Sat);
www.worthing.gov.uk/leisure

■ FOR CHILDREN

Brighton Sea Life Centre
Marine Parade.
Tel: 01273 604234;
www.sealifeeurope.com

Brighton Toy & Model Museum
Trafalgar Street (underneath railway station).
Tel: 01273 749494; www.brightontoymuseum.co.uk

Hove Museum & Art Gallery
19 New Church Road, Hove.
Tel: 03000 290900; www.brighton-hove-rpml.org.uk
Includes a wonderfully displayed toy gallery.

■ SHOPPING

BRIGHTON
High street stores are located in and around Churchill Square, Brighton's central shopping centre by Western Road. Individual clothing shops, jewellers and boutiques are in The Lanes, while the North Laine features exotic, arty and individual shopping.

Antiques Market
Brighton Marina.
Sun mornings.

Brighton Marina
www.brightonmarina.co.uk

Outlet shopping, discounts and end-of-line products.

Open Spaces
69 Trafalgar Street, Brighton.
Tel: 01273 600897
Outdoor equipment.

Surf and Ski
1–2 Regent Street, Brighton.
Tel: 01273 673192;
www.surfandski.co.uk

■ LOCAL SPECIALITIES

Farmers' Markets
Ralli Hall, Hove, 1st Sun of the month.
Friends' Meeting House, Ship Street, Brighton, 3rd Sat of the month.

■ PERFORMING ARTS

Brighton Centre
Kings Road.
Tel: 01273 290131
www.brightoncentre.co.uk
Gigs, ice shows and more, with top performers.

Brighton Dome
Church Street.
Tel: 01273 709709;
www.brightondome.org
Opera, ballet, orchestral and world music.

Komedia
44–47 Gardner Street, North Laine, Brighton.
Tel: 0845 293 8480;
www.komedia.co.uk
Top comedy/cabaret venue.

Pavilion Theatre
Marine Parade, Worthing.
Tel: 01903 206206;

www.worthingtheatres.co.uk
Venue on the pier.
Theatre Royal
New Road, Brighton.
Tel: 01273 764400;
www.ambassadortickets.com

■ **OUTDOOR ACTIVITIES**
BUS TOURS
Brighton City Sightseeing
01273 886200;
www.city-sightseeing.com
Open-top bus tours with
commentary
SPECTATOR SPORTS
Brighton and Hove Albion
Falmer.
Tel: 01273 695400;
www.seagulls.co.uk
Brighton Racecourse
Freshfield Road, Brighton.
Tel: 01273 603580; www.
brighton-racecourse.co.uk
Stages 20 race meetings
between Mar and Oct.
Sussex County Cricket Club
County Ground, Eaton Road,
Hove. Tel: 0871 282 2000;
www.sussexcricket.co.uk
Home of the oldest county
cricket club, which also plays
at Horsham and Arundel.
WATER & BEACH SPORTS
The Brighton Watersports
Company
West of Brighton Pier.
Tel: 01273 323160; www.
thebrightonwatersports.co.uk
Kayak hire and lessons,
doughnut rides,
wakeboarding, waterskiing,

parasailing, surf lessons,
watersports equipment.
Lagoon Watersports Centre
Hove Lagoon,
The Kingsway, Hove.
Tel: 01273 424842;
www.lagoon.co.uk
Powerboat driving,
windsurfing, sailing and
water skiing.
Ross Boat Trips
Pontoon 4, Brighton Marina.
Tel: 07836 262717;
www.watertours.co.uk
Boat trips and fishing trips
from the marina.
SailnetUK
Pontoon 19, West Jetty,
Brighton Marina.
Tel: 01273 628648;
www.sailnetuk.com
Sailing activities for
beginners.
Yellowave
Tel: 01273 672222;
www.yellowave.co.uk
Seafront sports on sand.

■ **ANNUAL EVENTS**
& CUSTOMS
Brighton
Brighton Festival,
three weeks in May. This
is the largest arts festival
in England.
Brighton Pride, Aug. Britain's
biggest gay and lesbian event.
Brighton & Hove Food &
Drink Festival, Mar and Sep.
City-centre market and other
gastronomic delights.

Brunswick Festival,
Aug. A Regency celebration.
Kite Flyers Festival, Jul.
London to Brighton Bike
Ride, Jun.
London to Brighton Veteran
Car Run, early Nov. Vintage
vehicles attempt the journey
from London, ending up on
the Kemp Town seafront.
Brighton Comedy Festival,
Oct.

Tea Rooms

Ditchling Tea Rooms

**West Street, Ditchling
BN6 8TS. Tel: 01273 842708**

Just opposite the church and popular with touring cyclists, this is like a cake shop with an attached warren of low-ceilinged old rooms in traditional tea-shop style. Alongside cream teas and cafetière coffees, it serves delicious all-day breakfasts, ploughman's and light lunches such as quiche and salad. You can also get wine and beer with your food.

Mock Turtle

**4 Pool Valley,
Brighton BN1 1NJ
Tel: 01273 327380**

Devotees of cream teas have been tucking in here since 1972. All the food is home-made, with tempting gateaux and meringues, and you can buy a pot of their jam to take home. Well placed near The Lanes and the Royal Pavilion, and next to the National Express bus terminus; expect a wait at busy times.

Pubs

Basketmakers Arms

**12 Gloucester Road,
Brighton BN1 4AD
Tel: 01273 689006**

A wide array of malt whiskies, several real ales and inexpensive bar food are hallmarks of this friendly back-street pub. The two bare-boarded rooms harbour a fascinating stash of old tins, advertisements, posters and cigarette cards. Not far from the Theatre Royal, this place is open all day, and there are some tables out on the pavement.

The Bull

**Ditchling BN6 8TA
Tel: 01273 843147**

In the centre of the village, this inn was revamped a few years ago, but has kept its character-laden bar much the same and there's usually a large fire blazing. The nicely mellow side rooms (used mainly by diners, though you can eat in the bar, too) are decorated with contemporary art. It's within striking distance of Ditchling Beacon and the view from the garden might inspire you to venture up there.

Fountain Inn

**Ashurst BN44 3AP
Tel: 01403 710219**

The village duckpond is next to this 16th-century free house. Food includes chargrilled steaks and burgers, and fish dishes such as sea bass. The bars are flagstoned and candlelit, and the big inglenook fireplace makes it cosily inviting; young children are not allowed inside the pub, but there's an attractive garden.

The Greys

**105 Southover Street,
Brighton BN2 9UA
Tel: 01273 680734;
www.greyspub.com**

The bar at this blue-painted street-corner pub is nicely straightforward, with basic furnishings, and a couple of real ales as well as an impressive Belgian beer selection. The shortish menu features very well presented food, partly French in style, and served in generous quantities. Live music one or two days a week; children are not allowed inside.

Royal Oak

**Wineham BN5 9AY
Tel: 01444 881252**

This tiled and half-timbered alehouse focuses on beer and atmosphere rather than food, with no piped music or similar contrivances. It's well worth the experience just coming here for a drink in the cottagey bar and to chat to the locals; wholesome locally sourced pub food is on offer. The floors are brick and bare boards, the furniture is agelessly rustic.

Lewes & Eastbourne

EASTBOURNE

The South Downs end spectacularly at the high chalk cliffs of the Seven Sisters and Beachy Head, the finest undeveloped stretch of coast in the southeast. Snuggled below the grassy slopes are sleepy one-street villages, country estates, the gracious but activity-packed resort of Eastbourne and the compact charm of the multi-layered town of Lewes. Further north are celebrated gardens, and the enchanting nostalgia fest that is the Bluebell Railway and the Winnie-the-Pooh landscapes of Ashdown Forest.

8 Walk start point

2 Cycle start point

2 Tour start point

BEACHY HEAD

Unmissable attractions

Explore the quirky architecture and speciality shops of Lewes and drink Harveys beer near the brewery itself...take an open-top bus up to Beachy Head or a boat to the foot of the cliffs...refresh yourself at Litlington Tea Garden after a hike over the Downs... puff through the landscape on a wonderfully preserved steam-hauled train on the Bluebell Railway and stop off at Sheffield Park, one of Britain's greatest gardens... learn to paraglide on the South Downs, the best training slopes in the country...go in-line skating for miles along Eastbourne's seafront.

1 Ashdown Forest
This open heathland area, a valuable habitat for many species of flora and fauna, is very popular with walkers and birders.

2 Bluebell Railway
Run by volunteers, the Bluebell Railway steams its way through the beautiful Sussex countryside from Sheffield Park Station.

3 Seven Sisters
The towering chalk cliffs, known as the Seven Sisters, are best viewed from the coastal path.

4 Cuckoo Trail
This popular cycling and walking trail follows part of a disused railway and links the towns of Heathfield, Hailsham and Polegate.

5 Eastbourne
Eastbourne's lengthy promenade and its grand Edwardian pier are both pleasant places for a stroll on a summer's day.

6 Beachy Head
Most fine days you'll see paragliders in action on the grassy, undulating downs and spectacular white cliffs of Beachy Head.

ALFRISTON MAP REF TQ5203

With its worn market cross and a flint church on a spreading village green, known as the Tye, Alfriston looks like the ideal English village – posters of the village fair were used to inspire British troops in the Second World War. In Sussex's smuggling days, it was a centre for illicit trading activity, but today the High Street with its narrow pavements has an enticing selection of speciality shops, pubs and tea rooms. If you can, go out of season to get more of the village atmosphere.

St Andrew's Church, built on a pre-Christian mound, dates from the 14th century, and is constructed from carefully squared flints. Inside it feels unusually wide and light. It's still in use for services and concerts: a 'musicians' gallery' was added in 1995 to provide extra space. The thatched, half-timbered Clergy House that lies by the green near the churchyard survived thanks to a far-sighted act of conservation in the 1896, when it became the very first building bought by the National Trust. It is a classic example of a Wealden Hall, with a delightful strip of cottage garden abutting the reedy fringes of the river. Inside, the building has been carefully restored to show its 14th-century fabric.

From the White Bridge, reached by a path running down the left side of the green looking at the church, you can stroll seawards for about a mile (1.6km) on the Kissing Gate Walk, along the Cuckmere River, crossing it at the next bridge near Litlington. Here the Harrow has a pleasant pub garden, and the lovely tea garden is a long-established local institution. Return along the other side.

A local curio within a ten-minute walk is the tiny Lullington Church. It's actually only a fragment of a church (just the chancel in fact), standing alone, but you can usually look inside: cross the footbridge at Alfriston, carry straight on along a path, over a road and on a further 400 yards (366m).

The light chalky soils and dry, sunny slopes of the South Downs make for excellent wine-growing conditions. The English Wine Centre, just off the A27 near Alfriston, stocks a good selection of 160 varieties of English wine alongside local preserves, fruit wines and beers. There are tutored wine tastings.

■ Visit

DRUSILLAS PARK

One of the top children's attractions in Sussex, Drusillas is an imaginative small zoo with lots of add-ons. There are cave-like interiors with child-friendly viewing of the smallest creatures, alternating with outside areas holding the larger animals like otters, meerkats and penguins. The route ends up in a huge adventure playground. Along the way there are plenty of hands-on activities that aim to blend the fun with the educational, such as the Zoolympics Challenge where children can rate their running and shouting performance against various animals. As you emerge into the playground and paddling area (extra charges for some activities) you get some idea of the origins of Drusillas as a pre-war tea rooms: the original cottage is still there. Birthday parties and animal adoption can be arranged, and there are special events such as summer visits from cartoon characters and weekends centred on reptiles or creepy-crawlies.

BENTLEY WILDFOWL & MOTOR MUSEUM
MAP REF TQ4916

There's an unexpected mixture of things at this country house and estate that's less conventional than you might expect. It is really the 20th-century creation of Gerald and Mary Askew. Gerald died in 1970 but Mary stayed on living here and made a gift of the house to the county. The Askews restored the old house, creating the Chinese Drawing Room, which features his collection of wildfowl paintings from Philip Rickman and a portrait of Gerald feeding his birds.

The pride and joy of the grounds is the remarkable collection of wildfowl, with more than 1,000 examples of exotic swans, geese and ducks (plus several similar bird types such as flamingos and cranes), and living in naturalistic enclosures. In all, Bentley is now home to 125 of the 147 species of wildfowl that are found anywhere on the planet. There's also a changing display of vintage motor cars and motorbikes from the early 1900s, lent by various owners; Bentley runs some Vehicle Event Days.

The Askews remodelled the garden, creating a number of 'rooms' with yew hedges as an extension of the house itself, and planted old roses, rare shrubs and trees. Further into the grounds are a nature trail, an adventure playground, a miniature railway and an assortment of shapely 'living willow' tunnels, domes, pathways and arbours. Children can enjoy orienteering courses, quiz sheets and Easter egg hunts. The shop includes crafts as well as bird-related items, and the old stable block houses a café.

BLUEBELL RAILWAY
MAP REF TQ4124

In 1960 this section of the old Lewes to East Grinstead line became the very first railway to be preserved as a heritage attraction, and its creators creamed off much of the best railwayana that was going – vintage locos, characterful carriages, signal boxes, goods stock, enamel advertising signs and all the other paraphernalia you would have seen at a country railway station in the days of steam. All the trains are steam powered. Good-value family tickets are available, and you can buy tickets for shorter sections of the trip. Thomas the Tank Engine creator Rev W Awdry based the Fat Controller on the man who was responsible for restoring this line in the late 1950s. Special days include Days Out With Thomas, Santa specials and Golden Arrow Pullman dining specials.

You don't have to be a train buff to enjoy a visit here. As the 9-mile (14.5km) trip from Kingscote ends at Sheffield Park, you can stroll from the southern terminus to see Sheffield Park Gardens (special combined tickets for visiting the Bluebell Railway and Sheffield Park Gardens or Standen are available) to complete a memorable day out. In early spring there are wonderful carpets of bluebells visible from the windows.

A bus shuttle service runs some days from East Grinstead mainline station to Kingscote (there's no road access), and through tickets can be purchased from mainline services for those wishing to join the Bluebell Railway. The next station, Horsted Keynes, is a good spot for viewing the scene from the platform.

From Firle Place

Stroll along the South Downs Way between Alfriston and the River Ouse and you can look down towards the sleepy village of West Firle, nestling in a patchwork of fields and hedgerows below the escarpment. At the centre of the village is Firle Place, home to the Gage family for over 500 years and now open to the public.

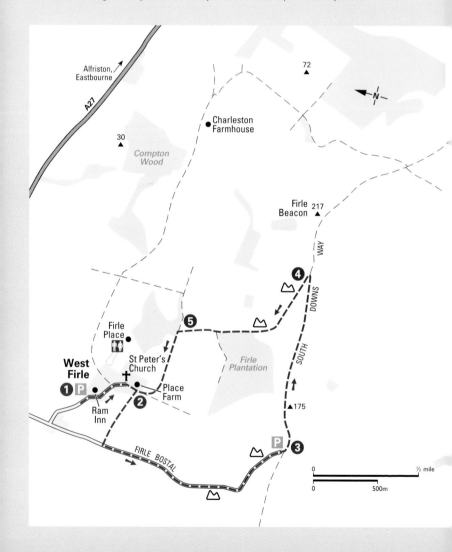

Route Directions

1 Turn left out of the car park, pass the Ram Inn and follow the road round to the right, through the village of Firle. Walk along to the village stores and a footpath to Charleston. Pass the turning to Firle's Church of St Peter and continue heading southwards, out of the village.

2 Turn right at a junction of concrete tracks and make for the road. Bear left, head for the downland escarpment and begin the long climb, steep in places. On reaching the car park at the top, swing left to a gate and join the South Downs Way.

3 Head eastwards on the long distance trail and, when you reach a blue-arrowed waymarker post, take a turn sharp left.

4 Follow the path in a north-westerly direction, down the steep slopes of the escarpment. On reaching a wooden post, where the path forks, take the lower grassy path and follow it as it descends in a wide sweep. Drop down to reach a gate and walk ahead, keeping a fence on the left. Skirt around Firle Plantation and follow the track all the way to the junction.

5 Bear left and walk along the track, keeping the dramatic escarpment on the left. As you approach the village of Firle, the track curves to the right towards the buildings of Place Farm. Cross over the junction of concrete tracks and retrace your steps back to the car park at the other end of the village.

Route facts

DISTANCE/TIME 4.25 miles (6.8km) 2h

MAP OS Explorer 123 South Downs Way: Newhaven to Eastbourne

START Free car park, West Firle; grid ref: TQ 468075

TRACKS Tracks, paths and roads.

GETTING TO THE START West Firle is signposted south off the A27 between Lewes and Eastbourne, 5 miles (8km) east of Lewes. Pass the entrance to Firle Place on the left, bearing slightly right. The entrance to the village car park is about 50yds (46m) further on, on the left.

THE PUB The Ram Inn, West Firle. Tel: 01273 858222

❶ Long, occasionally steep ascent and descent of the South Downs escarpment. It is best tackled by older family groups, as the walk is quite long.

Visit

THE LAVENDER LINE

Altogether on a smaller scale than the Bluebell Railway, but thoroughly enjoyable and possibly less overwhelming for smaller children, the volunteer-run Lavender Line (running along part of the old Lewes–Uckfield route) has steam and diesel locomotives that run along a short section of track from Isfield station, itself nicely done up with old advertising signs and furniture, and with a good-value buffet accessed from the platform. One ticket buys unlimited rides for the day, and there are regular special events.

Activity

WINDSURFING

You can see Britain's top windsurfers in action at Eastbourne during Eastbourne Extreme, a festival of sport held in July. This seaside resort is regarded as one of Britain's best venues for windsurfing. If you're tempted to have a go, the Watersports Centre (RYA accredited) in Royal Parade runs taster sessions and weekly courses. For the initial lesson, if you're a total beginner, you'll spend the day on Princes Park Lake before venturing into the sea. Hove Lagoon in Brighton and Hove is another good place to learn.

CHARLESTON FARMHOUSE

MAP REF TQ4807

Once inside this pebble-dashed and ivy-hung farmhouse, you are transported to the much-loved country retreat of artists Vanessa Bell (sister of Virginia Woolf) and Duncan Grant. They arrived in 1916 and made it their own for more than 60 years. While the house was shaken by the guns of the First World War in France, they began a long tradition of decorating the walls and furniture with their splashy, almost childlike designs.

They and their friends, known as the 'Bloomsbury Set', were determined to cast off Victorian conventions in many small ways, doing without table napkins and serving coffee instead of tea after dinner; and in radical ones: Grant's male lovers were regular guests, and Bell's husband Clive Bell – they never divorced – came to live with them in 1939.

Look for fascinating home-made details such as the beaded lampshades like upturned pottery colanders, or a woolly fringe concealing a radiator. The walled garden is a mass of cottagey planting and dense colour, and the well-stocked shop sells scarves, beads, pottery and painted furniture inspired by 'Bloomsbury', much of it made locally.

EASTBOURNE MAP REF TV6298

Though less obviously trendy than nearby Brighton, Eastbourne scores particularly strongly for its very appealing 4 miles (6.4km) of unspoiled seafront. The Dukes of Devonshire founded and still own much of the resort, and thanks partly to them it retains a gracious atmosphere, with rows of stucco-fronted hotels and guesthouses overlooking the beach (shingle with flat sands at low tide; safe for swimming), and striped directors' chairs set out for bandstand concerts. Eastbourne has made a real effort to keep up with the times, though: it hosts an exciting range of annual events such as the Airbourne air show, and is a great place for family fun and activities such as windsurfing and in-line skating.

Central to the seafront is the ornate Victorian pier, with its fairy lights strung between lamp-posts and some of the best surviving ironwork and little kiosks of the era, picked out in blue and white paint. The Dome at the end houses a fully restored camera obscura, built in 1901 and giving excellent views of what's happening outside projected on to a curved surface inside (it works best on a sunny day). Near by is the extraordinary turquoise flattened onion dome of the bandstand, opened in 1935. Its design owes more to the Brighton Pavilion than anything from the 20th century.

West from here you can stroll, join the skaters, or take the bus or seasonal hourly land train – the Dotto Train – past the Wish Tower (a Martello Tower) and the tiny Lifeboat Museum. Around this area the well-tended public gardens look sub-tropical; by the Wish Tower is a self-service cafeteria lounge with panoramic views. The promenade ends at the Holywell Tea Chalet, where there are huge stretches of rock pools at low tide. Just beyond, the Downs seem to slip into sea at the side of Beachy Head, and paths lead up to the top. Open-top buses in summer are another car-free and exhilarating way of reaching Beachy Head with regular hop-on, hop-off tours.

In the other direction, the Dotto Train runs along to Sovereign Harbour, Britain's largest man-made marina. Some of the housing here wouldn't look out of place in London's Docklands. There's a good range of waterfront restaurants and cafés with an international flavour, and harbour boat trips available. On the way you'll pass Princes Park, with mini golf, bowls, putting and a model boating lake. On Royal Parade, the Redoubt Fortress is a perfectly intact early 19th-century circular fort, now home to the Military Museum of Sussex. The museum has a huge array of uniforms, weapons, medals and photos, as well as Churchill's telescope. A model shows what the fortress was like when in use. The Sovereign Centre, has a large pool with slide, a wave machine and bubble pool. By the Devonshire Park Theatre, the Towner is a major venue for visual arts, and has exhibitions of contemporary and historic works.

The town's quirkiest attraction has to be How We Lived Then: the Museum of Shops, in Cornfield Terrace, a collection of some 100,000 items of bygone random merchandise. The museum started life as the childhood interest of Graham and Jan Upton, who still run it: they married in 1968, combined what items they had and accumulated more until eventually their entire house was taken over by their passion for the past. They now live in a flat upstairs while the other rooms are re-creations of yesteryear – a music shop with instruments, sheet music and old 78s, a tailor's shop, a draper's shop, a grocer's full of vintage packets and tins, and a wartime kitchen and living room with a 1940s family having tea.

Eastbourne's shopping possibilities includes the small independent shops of Grove Road's 'Little Chelsea' and the covered market-like Enterprise Shopping Centre near the railway station, and the large chain stores in the Arndale Centre and pedestrianised Terminus Road.

Hamsey & Barcombe Mills

Along this route of quiet lanes you'll find everything from Roman sites to wartime defences, and a mill pond and weirs. Off-road sections follow a disused railway track, with distant views of the South Downs, and an ancient 'green lane' that crosses fields and leads to the Lavender Line preserved steam railway. With three pubs to choose from along the way, there is plenty of choice for lunch or a drink.

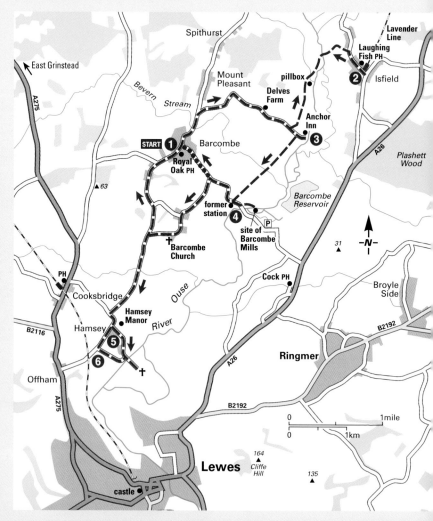

Route Directions

1 With the Royal Oak pub on your right, go along the main street in Barcombe and turn left in front of the village sign for 'The Anchor Inn' and Newick. At the bottom of the hill turn right on Boast Lane, signposted Anchor Inn. After passing Delves Farm, and just before a house on the right, look for a track beyond a gate on the left, into a triangular field. At the next triangular area, look to your left for a gate with a yellow arrow on it: at the far end of the field a line of hedgerow trees rising up to the top right skyline marks the line of a Roman road that ran from London to Lewes. Continue along the track, which later follows the left side of a field and passes a wartime brick pillbox. The route drops to a footbridge. Continue across a meadow to the gate ahead, up over another footbridge and along a track; ignore driveways to the right. At the road T-junction turn right into Isfield. Continue along past the Laughing Fish pub on your left to visit the Lavender Line preserved railway.

2 From Isfield retrace your route across the meadows and back past the pillbox. Turn left on the road to continue to The Anchor Inn.

3 Retrace your route a short distance from The Anchor Inn and, just before Keeper's Cottage on the left, turn left on the old railway track, signposted 'licensed bridleway to Barcombe Mills'.

4 On reaching a road opposite the old Barcombe Mills station, detour left and take the first road on the left. Turn right at the junction in front of the driveway to Barcombe House to reach the millpond and weirs of Barcombe Mills. Return the same way to the road, past Barcombe Mills station. At the next junction go straight ahead for a short-cut back into Barcombe. For the main route, turn left here, and pass Barcombe church. Carry on along the road, keeping left at the next two junctions towards Hamsey.

5 Just after Hamsey Manor turn left down Whitfeld Lane to Hamsey. There is a lovely half-timbered house called Yeoman's dated 1584; just after, turn left at a T-junction. The road crosses a former canal via a bridge. After the bridge, you can pick up the keys to Hamsey church from Pine Barn, the first house on the left. The road rises over the old railway to reach Hamsey church, a wonderful example of what medieval country churches used to look like. Return to Hamsey, keep left at the road junction by the canal bridge, past a pillbox.

6 Turn right at the T-junction. After Whitfeld Lane joins from the right follow signs for Barcombe to return to start.

Route facts

DISTANCE/TIME 12 miles (19.3km) 3h **ALTERNATIVE ROUTE** 4 miles (6.4km) 1h

MAP OS Explorer 122 South Downs Way: Steyning to Newhaven

START Barcombe village centre; roadside parking grid ref: TQ 418157

TRACKS Back lanes, hard stony track; extension along a track and through fields that get muddy after rain

GETTING TO THE START Barcombe is signposted from the A26 and A275, 4.3 miles (7km) north of Lewes.

CYCLE HIRE M's Cycle Hire 07852 986165; www.m-cyclehire.co.uk. Will deliver and pick up bikes free anywhere between Chichester and Lewes.

THE PUB The Anchor Inn, Barcombe. Tel: 01273 400414

❶ One short climb after Barcombe Mills, otherwise more gentle ups and downs. Take care on blind bends.

Cuckmere Haven and the Seven Sisters Country Park

Cuckmere Haven is one of the few undeveloped river mouths in the southeast. It was used by smugglers in the 18th century to bring ashore brandy and lace. The scene has changed little, with the eternal surge of waves breaking on the isolated shore. Cuckmere River joins the English Channel here but not before it makes a series of extraordinarily wide loops through water meadows. A stroll at Cuckmere Haven reveals the yellow horned-poppy and the fleshy leaved sea kale. Sea beet, curled dock and scentless camomile also grow here. The focal point of the lower valley is Seven Sisters Country Park, 692 acres (280ha) planned to blend with the coastal beauty of this area. There are artificial lakes and park trails, and a visitor centre with interesting exhibits and displays. Wildlife plays a key role, providing naturalists with many hours of enjoyment. The flowers and insects here are at their best in early to mid-summer, while spring and autumn are a good time for views of migrating birds.

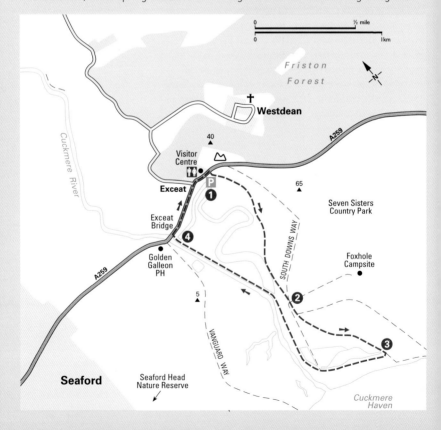

Route Directions

1 Make for the gate situated near the entrance to the Seven Sisters Country Park and follow the wide, grassy path towards the beach. The path gradually curves to the right, running alongside a concrete track. The Cuckmere River meanders beside you, heading for the open sea. Continue ahead between the track and the river and make for a South Downs Way sign.

2 Avoid the long distance trail as it runs in from the left, pass it and the Foxhole campsite and keep ahead, through the gate towards the beach. Veer left at the beach and South Downs Way sign. On reaching the next gate, don't go through it. Instead, keep right and follow the beach sign. Pass a couple of wartime pill boxes on the left, an evocative reminder of less peaceful times, and go through a gate. Join a stony path and walk ahead to the beach, with the white wall of the Seven Sisters rearing up beside you.

3 Turn right and cross the shore, approaching a Cuckmere Haven Emergency Point sign. Branch off to the right to join another track here. Follow this for about 50yds (46m) until you come to a junction and keep left, following the Park Trail. Keep beside the Cuckmere, the landscape here is characterised by a network of meandering channels and waterways, all feeding into the river. Pass a turning for Foxhole campsite and follow the footpath as it veers left, in line with the Cuckmere. Make for a kissing gate and continue on the straight path by the side of the river.

4 Keep ahead to the road at Exceat Bridge and on the left is the Golden Galleon pub. Turn right and follow the A259 to return to the car park at the country park.

Route facts

DISTANCE/TIME 3 miles (4.8km) 1h30

MAP OS Explorer 123 South Downs Way: Newhaven to Eastbourne

START Fee-paying car park opposite the Seven Sisters Country Park visitor centre, at Exceat; grid ref: TV 518995

TRACKS Grassy trails and well-used paths; mostly beside the Cuckmere or canalised branch of river.

GETTING TO THE START The visitor centre for the Seven Sisters Country Park is just east of the turning at Exceat on the A259 which is signed to Westdean and Alfriston. Park on the south side of the A259, by the green phone box.

THE PUB Golden Galleon, Exceat Bridge. Tel: 01323 892247

❶ This walk is suitable for children of all ages.

GLYNDE MAP REF TQ4608

This is still very much an estate village, owned by Glynde Place, the Elizabethan manor house just north. As well as a tea room and pub with a large garden (the Trevor Arms), the village also has its own smithy. Bearing the date of 1907 by its horseshoe-shaped doorway, this has an assortment of tools hanging over a pair of brick-built hearths; the smith makes various types of ironwork.

A signposted path leading off from a stile roughly opposite the Little Cottage Tea Room on Ranscombe Lane takes visitors up Mount Caburn. You will often notice paragliders hovering gracefully over this summit, which looks down the Ouse valley towards the sea. Chalk-loving wild flowers proliferate on the steep slopes, and the site is encircled with large Saxon and Iron Age ramparts.

Glynde Place is screened from the road by the stable block situated next to a Palladian-style church. The flint gables and brick chimneys at the front are from Tudor times, the back section was added in 1760. Knowledgeable guides introduce visitors to the family history, and with a welcome absence of roping-off you can get up close to all the details, including miniatures and embroidery. The walls are hung with old masters brought back from an Italian Grand Tour – the efforts of 300 years of collecting by the (related) Morley, Trevor and Brand families. Stone wyverns crown the gates beyond the Coach House, where the Tea Room has a cobbled courtyard shaded by fruit trees.

North of the village is Glyndebourne Opera House, home to Britain's top country house opera company.

LEWES MAP REF TQ4608

You can hardly fail to be aware of the landscape as you wander around this enticing town, perched steeply on a hill between great rises of the Downs, with the River Ouse winding its way through adjacent water meadows.

A rich variety of building materials has been used in Lewes – much of which was brought in by the river in the town's days as a busy port – with various uses of flint, brick, timber, stone, tiles, and red or black sham bricks called mathematical tiles, that were added to timber façades in the 18th century to upgrade houses to a more contemporary look (you can spot them all over town: the giveaways are the wooden corners on the buildings, and the unevenness of the façades when you look upwards).

Today Lewes is occupied by a lively mixture of loyal natives and more recent converts, with a high percentage of artists, academics, book designers and writers. Look for the smart boutiques and arty shops in the upper High Street. Classy gifts and homewares are found in the shops in the Old Needlemakers, a red-brick Victorian factory saved from demolition in the 1980s, and interesting antiques and secondhand book dealers are dotted all over town.

The castle crowns an artificial mound which may be prehistoric in date, like Brack Mount, on the other side of the castle precincts. There's not a great deal inside, but it provides a fascinating view of Lewes' complicated layout, with tiny lanes – known as twittens, and mostly laid out in Saxon times – sloping down from a long, high street lined with

■ Insight

LEWES BONFIRE

Shop windows are boarded up as Lewes prepares for the biggest 5 November celebrations in Britain. Bonfire societies from all over Sussex arrive with banners and marching bands to join the Lewes societies in a grand procession around town, with 'bonfire boys' in hooped sweaters or elaborate fancy dress, and agricultural bird scarers known as 'rookies' exploding with ear-splitting volume as the torchlit procession makes its way from one end of town to the other. Wreaths are placed with great ceremony at the war memorial, and burning barrel races take place towards the River Ouse. Late in the evening, huge firework displays take place at the Lewes societies' sites on the edge of the town. The Bonfire Societies stress that what they chiefly celebrate on this night is freedom, independence and resisting being dictated to by outsiders – the unofficial motto of Sussex being 'We won't be druv!'

historic buildings, many of which look Georgian at the front but much older behind. Beyond the moat, you might spot the studio extending out of the back of Reeves, the world's oldest high street photographer's, established 1840.

William the Conqueror's brother-in-law built the castle here to show the locals that the Normans meant business and firmly held the reins of power. The imposing barbican was added mostly for show later on and was never used in a military situation, but behind it is a plainer rounded arch that straddles the cobbled lane and is part of the Norman structure. The Normans also built a

huge priory which was still a substantial ruin after the Dissolution: local outrage when the new Lewes-to-Brighton railway destroyed much of what survived served to galvanise a group of people into forming the Sussex Archaeological Society in 1848. The society took over the castle and other local endangered buildings, and predated the National Trust as a conservation body. Entrance to the castle includes the museum in Barbican House, the headquarters of the Sussex Archaeological Society, with its glass cases full of prehistoric flints, Sussex pottery and other archaeological finds. On every half hour you can watch the Town Model sound and light show – a painstakingly created model of Lewes in around 1830 with a commentary leading you through the town's story.

Cobbled Keere Street dips abruptly from the timber-framed secondhand bookshop on the High Street, down to Southover Grange – a rather Cotswoldy-looking stone-built house created from stone that was taken from the priory and now owned by the town. The garden just behind it is a favourite open space for Lewesians, with bright bedding plants, stone arches, an ancient mulberry tree and gorgeous views up to the castle; in summer you can enjoy teas, soft drinks and a range of cakes on sale here from a booth by the lawn.

Southover High Street has some of the choicest historic houses in town, among them Anne of Cleves House (also owned by the Sussex Archaeological Society), a tile-hung timber-framed house given to Anne of Cleves as part of her divorce settlement from Henry VIII.

She never lived there, but it's well worth a look, with an antiquated bedroom, lots of iron firebacks made when the Weald was a major centre of iron-making, and a room of Lewes artefacts.

By the River Ouse at the bottom of town, Harvey's Brewery – housed within a splendid rambling Victorian building affectionately known to locals as Lewes Cathedral – often exudes a wholesome malty smell during the brewing process. You can buy Harvey's beer, and other brewery related products, at the brewery shop and also at the John Harvey pub, down an alley opposite.

MICHELHAM PRIORY
MAP REF TQ5609

Cross the stone bridge over the longest water-filled moat in England and peep through the archway of a perfect stone gateway. You will see before you the lovingly cared-for gardens and low grey buildings of a house, which has evolved over nearly 800 years from a religious foundation to a country home to a visitor attraction. It's the peaceful atmosphere of the place and its setting in gently rolling woods and fields that is the main attraction rather than any one feature. Michelham hosts a popular series of regular events – medieval weekends, gardening and country fairs and so on. The field on the far side of the moat is used for archaeological experiments and reconstructions, such as iron-smelting, and building round houses. Don't miss the fully working watermill, found just off the car park, which is in action every afternoon. You can pick up a bag of your own stoneground flour from the shop.

NEWHAVEN & SEAFORD
MAP REF TQ4502

As a busy working port, Newhaven is not an obviously enticing place, but it has a characterful stretch of riverside on the west side leading down to Newhaven Fort and the sea, and a growing colony of artists from Brighton looking for cheaper workspace. There has been some redevelopment, but that has not eroded the salty feeling of the quayside with its fishing boats, weathered wooden jetties, tarred ropes and hungry-looking gulls. Park the car at the end of the road, watch the ferries, walk out among the fishermen on the breakwater and go onto one of two beaches backed by cliffs.

The cliffs are dotted with holes that hint at the presence of Newhaven Fort with its tunnels and gun emplacements. To visit, take the road on the right as you head for the seafront. In use up to the 1950s, the fort has grassy slopes, tunnels and items of military hardware. In the arches around the courtyard are a range of exhibitions, with a huge cache of material from both of the world wars, including films of D-Day and a lively re-creation of a blitzed street. There's usually something on at weekends – military tattoos, rock concerts, plays and model shows, but the largest event is the Battle of Britain commemoration held on the weekend nearest 17 September, with military vehicles and people in 1940s dress.

The shingle beach extends along to Seaford, and it's all uncommercialised. On hot afternoons in summer this whole stretch is a locals' playground – one of the nearest beaches to London (with trains to Bishopstone and Seaford), but scarcely well known. The beach shelves steeply and often has a strong drift, so swim with care. There's a local museum in the Martello Tower at the far Seaford end, forming the westernmost tower of a chain of coastal defences built in the Napoleonic Wars. Beyond here you can walk steeply up onto Seaford Head, for a superb view of the Seven Sisters.

RODMELL MAP REF TQ4207

Although most visitors come for Monk's House, the Sussex home of Bloomsbury novelist Virginia Woolf and her husband Leonard, Rodmell deserves a look in its own right as one of the prettiest of the chain of villages off the unclassified road between Lewes and Newhaven. Its loop-shaped road leads past a great variety of buildings: Deep Thatch Cottage on the right is aptly named and the Old Rectory has a handsome flint frontage.

'There is little ceremony or precision at Monk's House. It is an unpretending house, long and low, a house of many doors' wrote Virginia in her diary in 1919. The house is set deep in the earth, surrounded by a lovingly tended cottage garden, and its green-painted sitting room feels almost underwater: it is full of reminders of the Woolfs' literary lives. They used Monk's House as their country base from 1919, visiting Virginia's sister's household at Charleston. Virginia wrote in the summer house in the orchard, where you can see her desk and her bottle of green ink. Virginia's depression returned and in 1941 she drowned herself in the nearby Ouse. Leonard lived on here until 1969.

SEVEN SISTERS & BEACHY HEAD MAP REF TV5298

A rollercoaster of turf-capped white cliffs undulates between Seaford and Eastbourne, rising to seven mini-peaks or 'sisters' known as the Seven Sisters – a spectacular reminder that Britain was once joined to France before the two countries were broken apart by the Channel, which continues to erode the sheer, crumbling chalk heights. With Seaford Head to the west and Beachy Head to the east, this makes up the longest and most scenic stretch of undeveloped coast in southeast England.

The Seven Sisters Country Park encompasses the western part of the cliffs. Two large car parks either side of the A259 at Exceat (café, shop, cycle hire and visitor centre here) give access into Friston Forest to the north and also Cuckmere Haven where the meandering Cuckmere River meets the sea. This is the only undeveloped estuary in Sussex, with wildlife thriving in the meadows, reed beds and ponds. As you approach the beach you pass an artificial lagoon, made in 1975, and a nesting and feeding area for birds. A metalled path leads from the road, suitable for wheelchairs, cycles and pushchairs, and you can join the chalk path up onto the Seven Sisters themselves near the sea. From the beach (shingle and shelves quite steeply, so this is for stronger swimmers only) there is a glorious view along the bottom of the Seven Sisters to the left and up to the cottages on Seaford Head to the right. During the Second World War a mock town, with lights, was built here to mislead enemy bombers into bombing

Activity

FRISTON FOREST

The Seven Sisters Country Park at Exceat adjoins Friston Forest, laced with paths and mountain bike routes (from easy to challenging). Although it's relatively new, with a plantation of mainly beech, Scots and Corsican pine – created from 1926 and planted on an underground reservoir that serves Eastbourne – it does harbour a variety of wildlife. Tread quietly and you might spot adders, badgers, roe deer or foxes, and there are rare butterflies like fritillaries, white admirals and clouded yellows. Surrounded by the forest is the remote-feeling village of Westdean. There's no parking in the village, so walk up the signposted route from the Seven Sisters Country Park car park.

Visit

SEVEN SISTERS SHEEP CENTRE

Just south of East Dean the road towards Birling Gap passes the Seven Sisters Sheep Centre. This is one of the world's largest sheep collections, a working farm with more than 40 different sheep breeds and other farm animals; also shearing, milking, cheese making and spinning demonstrations, plus a tea room and picnic site. A must for children, with many young animals to feed and cuddle.

Visit

THE MILLENNIUM SEED BANK

A recent groundbreaking concept at Wakehurst has been the establishment of the Millennium Seed Bank Project, in a futuristic pavilion-like structure near the house. There's an exhibition on what they're aiming to do here, and you can see into the laboratories where the work is being carried out to store a worldwide collection of seeds in a bid to safeguard 24,000 plant species from all over the world from extinction.

this instead of Newhaven; there are still fortifications here, including concrete 'dragon teeth' tank traps seen to the right, just before the beach.

You can also reach the Seven Sisters from the car park at Crowlink (take the small road leading south by the pond at Friston) and from East Dean, which has a free car park just south of the A259, next to the spreading village green by the renowned Tiger Inn.

East of the Seven Sisters at Birling Gap, steps lead down to the shore, and there are rock pools to explore at low tide, though the sharp flinty surfaces are hard underfoot for bathers. The buildings here are threatened by the sea – two of the coastguard cottages have been demolished for safety reasons – and there has been a long debate about their future. For more views of the Seven Sisters, a path rises up the hill to Belle Tout, 'the lighthouse that moved'. The sea is eroding the cliff back a bit every year, and in 1999 this former lighthouse (today a private house) had to be moved away from the cliff edge, using special rails, an event that appeared on TV worldwide. You can get an idea of the scale of the erosion by seeing the scary proximity of the road to the cliff edge just after Belle Tout.

Further east is Beachy Head, the highest point on the Sussex coast. This sheer chalk cliff plummets a full 534 feet (163m), with a lighthouse on the shore far below. The views up here are dizzying in the extreme (on a clear day you can see Dungeness to the east and the Isle of Wight to the west), but do be careful as the cliff edge is not stable. From

Eastbourne, the South Downs Way leads up – or you can continue along the undercliff closer to the shore before a steep final ascent. From Terminus Road or from the pier in the town centre hop on an open-topped City Sightseeing bus, that will take you up the zig-zagging road (they don't run in winter). For a close-up of the cliffs from below, take a boat tour (summer, daytime and evening). They leave from two places in Eastbourne: one boat goes from just west of the pier, and a restored lifeboat departs from Sovereign Harbour (the latter also goes to Royal Sovereign Light Tower). Ask staff at the Tourist Information Centre in Eastbourne for details of guided walks and bike rides with a downland ranger.

SHEFFIELD PARK GARDEN
MAP REF TV5298

This 120-acre (48ha) garden and arboretum is overlooked by a Gothic mansion (now divided into private flats) and was landscaped by the renowned 'Capability' Brown. It has a supremely restful character with four linked lakes providing constantly changing vistas. Rhododendrons and azaleas combine to create a vivid spectacle in early summer (late May and early June), while in the autumn the foliage from the many rare trees and shrubs bursts into stunning colours and brings visitors from far around. Visitors with disabilities can make use of self-drive battery-powered vehicles, available free of charge. It's a short walk along the road from Sheffield Park station, at the southern terminus of the Bluebell Railway, and joint tickets for both attractions are available.

WAKEHURST PLACE
MAP REF TQ3432

Gerald Loder, also known as Lord Wakehurst, bought this 180-acre (73ha) estate in 1903 and he and his successor, Sir Henry Price, lavished their gardening expertise on it until it passed into the hands of the Royal Botanic Gardens, Kew, in 1965. There's huge interest here, whether you seek inspiration for your own garden or just wish to drink in the atmosphere. There's a winter garden, in summer the specimen beds and the walled garden are a riot of colour, while autumn brings seasonal tints to the foliage. Hardy plants are arranged according to geographical region – the Southern Hemisphere Garden includes groupings from South Africa, New Zealand, Australia and South America, and there are National Collections of hypericums, skimmias, birches and southern beeches. Beyond the mansion (not open) and café, the ground dips into a valley, which then winds past the Bog Garden, through the delightfully named Iris Dell, and around a deep glade which is planted with species that flourish in the Himalayas. At the far corner of the estate, the Loder Valley reserve is a wetland area rich in wildlife and wild plants, but access is limited. There are guided walks around the estate, and entertaining nuggets of information are helpfully posted on boards.

WEST FIRLE MAP REF TQ4707
Turn off the A27 into West Firle (Firle on some maps) and you're in a different world. Beyond the gatehouse proudly announcing the entrance to Firle Place

■ Activity

WALK TO

Paths lead up to above the Long Man where there is some glorious walking undisturbed by sounds from the modern world, skirting the spectacular dry valley of Deep Dean. Turn left below the Long Man, then right at a waymarked path that goes steeply upwards. You can head southwards to Lullington Heath National Nature Reserve, a very unusual mixture of chalk downland and acid heath with acid-loving plants such as heathers and tormentil alongside chalk-tolerant dropwort, thyme and salad burnet.

lies a timeless estate village – with the flint-fronted cottages owned by Firle Place itself. Near the Ram Inn and by the high wall of the kitchen garden, the village street turns right past a lane leading to the church, notable for its coloured stained glass by John Piper, and its Gage family monuments.

Firle Place has been the home of the Gages for nearly half a millennium. The original owner, Sir John Gage, bought the site in 1530. The house he developed was Tudor: the creamy, French-looking façade was created in the 18th century with Caen stone brought from Lewes Priory. It's hidden from view until you are almost upon it: tucked into a hollow beneath the South Downs, with its gardens sloping up behind. The 18th-century refurbishments with pastel-washed walls and delicate plasterwork give the house a light and liveable feel: the cream-and-gold pillared drawing room has well-used board games and records alongside the old masters; a

Victorian anteroom has been left as it was in 1840. Views extend over the park from the Long Gallery upstairs and the tea room terrace, alongside the Billiard Room and shop, and there are often special events in the grounds.

A road out of the village leads up to the top of the Downs, where you can walk the South Downs Way to Firle Beacon and a neolithic long barrow.

WILMINGTON   MAP REF TQ5404

As you come into this village, tucked under the Downs between Lewes and Eastbourne, you see the Giant's Rest pub. This refers to the 235-foot (71m) tall chalk carving known as the Long Man of Wilmington, who comes into view as you leave the far end of the village. The church has a 1,000-year yew tree thought to be Sussex's oldest tree. From the car park and toilets just beyond, you can cross the over road onto a path that leads to just below the Long Man, which in latter years has been outlined with white-painted blocks. This is the largest hill carving in Britain: no one knows when or why it was created, and it has been variously explained as a fertility symbol, a surveyor of ley lines (holding two staffs) or a Roman or Anglo-Saxon figure. Perhaps the greatest mystery is that there are no written records of the figure existing at all before 1710. Recent archaeological work suggests that it may date from the Tudor period, some time between 1500 and 1600, when new landowners taking over monastery sites like nearby Wilmington Priory were sometimes keen to put their own mark on the land with pagan-looking figures.

Lewes, Wakehurst Place and Ashdown Forest

This route celebrates Sussex in all its diversity: starting from Lewes, beautifully set in the South Downs, it heads into the Weald. You encounter the primaeval-feeling heathlands and woods of the Ashdown Forest – the landscape of the immortal Winnie-the-Pooh stories – and pass some of the world's greatest gardens and the terminus of the Bluebell Railway, one of Britain's most engaging steam railways. Near the end you can finish in high style by driving up on to the Downs for a view far across southern England. There's no shortage of good pubs and tea rooms along the route where you can stop and take a break and a bite to eat.

Route Directions

1 Leave the historic county town of Lewes on the A275. Cross the A272 at North Chailey and continue on the A275. You pass Sheffield Park station, the southern terminus of the Bluebell Railway on the left. A short distance on is the entrance to Sheffield Park Garden.
You can detour ahead a short distance to Heaven Farm, on the left of the A275, which is a delightfully informal spot for lunch or tea.

2 Just after the entrance to Sheffield Park Garden, turn right on a minor road to Fletching, where the Griffin Inn also makes an excellent lunch spot. Carry on to the A272, turn left to Maresfield, left at the A22, and at the next roundabout turn off to the B2026. This climbs over Ashdown Forest, keeping left at a fork with the B2188. The sandy tracks, rolling heaths and clumps of

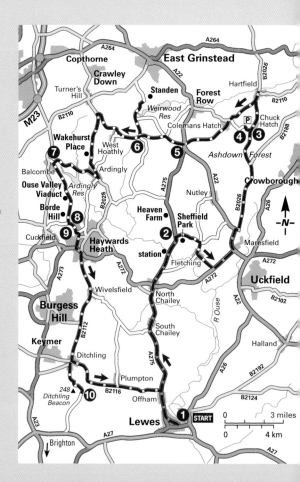

pine trees make a remote landscape. It was here that A A Milne set his Winnie-the-Pooh stories, and the scene is instantly familiar from E H Shephard's illustrations. It's vintage territory for picnics (with plentiful car parks), kite flying and bracing walks.

3 At Chuck Hatch you can detour left along a lane for the Poohsticks Bridge, which featured in Milne's stories. Soon you see the entrance to Pooh car park on the right. The path leading from the car park goes through the woods, and at a corner of the road, turn right on a bridleway that leads down to the bridge. Though rebuilt since Milne's time, the bridge looks exactly like the original structure where Pooh and his friends enjoyed a game of poohsticks.

4 Return to the B2026 and continue to Hartfield. A shop here called Pooh Corner has a wide array of Pooh-related gifts. Take the B2110 west from Hartfield towards Forest Row, then take the second left turn past Coleman's Hatch, keeping forward by the weatherboarded Hatch pub (with a very pretty garden). You pass the Ashdown Forest Centre on your right, which has a display and information about the forest.

5 Cross the A22 and take the minor road opposite, turning left at the next crossroads towards West Hoathly. At the next crossroads detour right past the end of Weirwood Reservoir to Standen house (National Trust).
This highly unusual Arts and Crafts house was designed by Philip Webb, a friend and associate of William Morris; the gardens have views over the Weald.

6 Carry on to the B2028, turn left along it, past the entrance to Wakehurst Place, which is maintained by the Royal Botanic Gardens at Kew, and home to the Millennium Seed Bank. Turn right at Ardingly, towards Balcombe, past Ardingly church and over one arm of Ardingly Reservoir.
This body of water looks almost natural, and provides scope for waterside strolls, as well as fishing and water sports such as canoeing, windsurfing and sailing.

7 Turn left at the edge of Balcombe, and continue towards Haywards Heath.
On the left you see the huge Ouse Valley Viaduct, which carries the London–Brighton railway. A footpath leads from the road and disappears underneath the structure, from which point you can

appreciate an extraordinary view through all the oval spaces in the piers.

8 Further on along the same road are Borde Hill gardens.
This is an informal creation of parkland and woods, with a spectacular show of blooms during early summer when the rhododendrons and azaleas are out.

9 After Borde Hill gardens, turn left on a minor road and take the A272 to Haywards Heath, then the B2112 to Ditchling. The old village nestles at the foot of the South Downs (the Bull makes a welcoming stopping place, in addition to a couple of tea rooms), and from there detour south on the road signposted to Ditchling Beacon.
From the car park at the top you can take a short stroll along the South Downs Way, enjoying the sweeping views over the Weald.

10 Return to Ditchling and go east along the B2116 to join the A275 just outside Lewes.

A Circuit from Wilmington

One of Britain's most impressive and enduring mysteries is the focal point of this glorious walk high on the Downs. Cut into the turf below Windover Hill, the chalk figure of the Long Man of Wilmington is the largest representation of the human figure in western Europe and yet it remains an enigma, its origins shrouded in mystery. For centuries experts have been trying to solve this ancient puzzle, but no one has been able to prove who he is or what he symbolises. The walk passes as close as it can to the Long Man before heading out into the isolated downland country. The return route back to Wilmington takes in part of the South Downs Way.

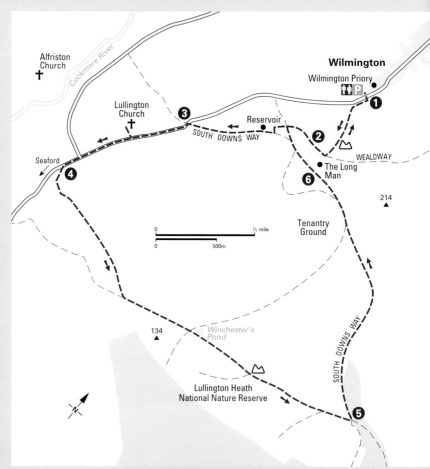

Route Directions

1 Make for the car park exit and follow the path parallel to the road, heading towards the Long Man of Wilmington. Bear left at the stile and take the Wealdway to the chalk figure. Climb quite steeply, curving to the right. Go through a gate, avoid the Wealdway arrow and go straight ahead towards the escarpment, veering right just below the figure of the Long Man.

2 Go through the next gate, cross a track and bear left on reaching a fence. A few paces brings you to a gate and a sign for the South Downs Way. Turn right, pass a small reservoir and follow the track to the road.

3 Turn left and walk down to a signpost for Lullington church, following the path alongside several cottages. After visiting the church, retrace your steps to the road and turn right. Head down the lane and look for Alfriston church on the right. Pass a turning to the village on the right and continue ahead towards Seaford. Look out for a post box and swing left here, signposted 'Jevington'.

4 Follow the bridleway as it climbs steadily between tracts of remote downland. Keep left at the next main junction and there is a moderate climb. Avoid the bridle track branching off to the left and continue ahead towards Jevington. Lullington Heath National Nature Reserve is on the right now. Pass a bridleway on the right and keep on the track as it climbs steeply. Pass a second sign and also a map for the nature reserve and make for a junction with the South Downs Way.

5 Turn left and follow the enclosed path to a gate. Go straight ahead alongside woodland and pass through a second gate. The path begins a gradual curve to the left and eventually passes along the rim of a spectacular dry valley known as Tenantry Ground. Keep the fence on your left and look for a gate ahead. Swing right as you approach it to a stile and then follow the path alongside the fence, crossing along the top of the Long Man.

6 Glance to your right and you can just make out the head and body of the chalk figure down below. It's an intriguing view. Continue keeping the fence on the right and descend to a gate. Turn right

Route facts

TIME/DISTANCE 6.25 miles (10.1km) 2h30

MAP OS Explorer 123 South Downs Way: Newhaven to Eastbourne

START Long-stay car park, Wilmington (free); grid ref: TQ 543042

TRACKS Downland paths and tracks, stretch of country road, 1 stile.

GETTING TO THE START Wilmington is signposted south off the A27 between Lewes and Eastbourne, 2 miles (3.2km) west of Polegate. Drive through the village to locate the car park, which is on the right at the top of the hill.

THE PUB The Giant's Rest, Wilmington. Tel: 01323 870207

❶ Although quite long, this walk is generally easy and suitable for experienced children of all ages.

here and retrace your steps to the start in the car park at Wilmington.

■ TOURIST INFORMATION CENTRES

Eastbourne
Cornfield Road.
Tel: 0871 663 0031;
www.visiteastbourne.com

Lewes
187 High Street.
Tel: 01273 483448

Seaford
37 Church Street.
Tel: 01323 897426

■ PLACES OF INTEREST

Beachy Head Countryside Centre
Tel: 01323 737273;
www.beachyhead.org.uk

Bentley Wildfowl and Motor Museum
Halland. Tel: 01825 840573;
www.bentley.org.uk

Filching Manor Motor Museum
Wannock, nr Polegate.
Tel: 01323 487838

Firle Place
Tel: 01273 858307;
www.firleplace.co.uk

Glynde Place
Tel: 01273 858224;
www.glyndeplace.com

Michelham Priory
Tel: 01323 844224;
www.sussexpast.co.uk

Monk's House
Rodmell.
Tel: 01323 870001;
www.nationaltrust.org.uk

Nymans Garden
Handcross, nr Haywards
Heath. Tel: 01444 400321;
www.nationaltrust.org.uk

Paradise Park
Off A26 north of Newhaven.
Tel: 01273 512123;
www.paradisepark.co.uk
Gardens, garden centre, heritage trail, dinosaurs and local history museum.

Redoubt Fortress and Military Museum
Royal Parade, Eastbourne.
Tel: 01323 410300

RidgeView Estate Winery
Fragbarrow Lane, Ditchling Common. Tel: 01444 241441;
www.ridgeview.co.uk

Seven Sisters Country Park
Exceat. Tel: 01323 870280;
www.sevensisters.org.uk

Sheffield Park Garden
Tel: 01825 790231;
www. nationaltrust.org.uk

Standen
Tel: 01342 323029;
www.nationaltrust.org.uk
Arts and crafts home.

Wakehurst Place
Ardingley.
Tel: 01444 894066;
www.kew.org

■ FOR CHILDREN

Ashdown Forest Llama Park
Wych Cross, Forest Row.
Tel: 01825 712040;
www.llamapark.co.uk

Bluebell Railway
Sheffield Park Station.
Tel: 01825 720800;
www.bluebell-railway.co.uk

Drusillas Park
Alfriston. Tel: 01323 874100;
www.drusillas.co.uk

Eastbourne Miniature Steam Railway Adventure Park
Lottbridge Drove, Eastbourne.
Tel: 01323 520229;
www.emsr.co.uk

Fort Fun
Royal Parade, Eastbourne.
Tel: 01323 642833;
www.fortfun.co.uk
Indoor and outdoor fun.

Knockhatch Adventure Park
Hailsham. Tel: 01323 442051;
www.knockhatch.com
Includes go-karts and dry-ski slope.

Lavender Line
Isfield. Tel: 01825 750515;
www.lavender-line.co.uk

Newhaven Fort
Tel: 01273 517622;
www.newhavenfort.org.uk

Seven Sisters Sheep Centre
South of East Dean.
Tel: 01323 423302;
www.sheepcentre.co.uk

■ SHOPPING

The largest shopping town is Eastbourne, with major retail chains represented. Lewes has a good variety of speciality shopping, including antiques and second-hand books, and Alfriston has a range of village gift shops. Newhaven is good for chandlery and fish.

FARMERS MARKETS

Held in the morning

Eastbourne

Community Wise, Ocklynge Road, Old Town, last Sat of month.

East Dean

Village hall, Wed.

Hailsham

Cattle market, 2nd Sat of month.

Lewes

Precinct, 1st Sat of month.

■ LOCAL SPECIALITIES

English Wine Centre

Tel: 01323 870164; www.englishwine.co.uk Off A27 nr Alfriston.

Harveys Brewery Shop

Cliffe High Street, Lewes. Tel: 01273 480217; www.harveys.org.uk

Middle Farm

On A27 at Firle, nr Lewes, Tel: 01323 811324/811411; www.farm-shop.co.uk Farm shop and English Farm Cider Centre.

■ PERFORMING ARTS

Bandstand

Grand Parade, Eastbourne. Tel: 01323 410611; www.eastbournebandstand.co.uk

Congress Theatre

Compton Street, Eastbourne. Tel: 01323 412000; www.eastbournetheatres.co.uk Musicals, comedy, opera, ballet and concerts.

Devonshire Park Theatre

Compton Street, Eastbourne. Tel: 01323 412000; www.eastbournetheatres.co.uk

Glyndebourne Opera House

Tel: 01273 813813; www.glyndebourne.com

Royal Hippodrome

112 Seaside Road, Eastbourne. Tel: 01323 412000; www.eastbournetheatres.co.uk

■ OUTDOOR ACTIVITIES

BOAT TRIPS

Allchorn Pleasure Boats, The Promenade, Eastbourne. Tel: 01323 410606; www.allchornpleasureboats.co.uk

CYCLE HIRE

Seven Sisters Cycle Company

Next to Seven Sisters Country Park Visitor Centre, Exceat. Tel: 01323 870310; www.cuckmere-cycle.co.uk

HANG-GLIDING & PARAGLIDING

Airworks

Glynde Station. Tel: 01273 858108; www.airworks.co.uk Courses, taster days etc. Sussex Hang Gliding & Paragliding Glynde. On the A27. Tel: 01273 858170; www.sussexhgpg.co.uk Full courses and taster days are available.

■ ANNUAL EVENTS & CUSTOMS

Ardingly

South of England Show, Ardingly Showground, Jun.

Bentley

Bentley Wildfowl and Motor Museum, Weald WoodFair. Mid-Sep. Three-day festival.

Charleston

Charleston Festival. Late May, alongside the Brighton Festival, literary events/talks.

Eastbourne

Airbourne. Four-day air festival. Beachy Head is a good vantage point. Mid-Aug. Eastbourne Extreme, Jul. Windsurfing, parasailing, land yachting, inline skating. Eastbourne Beer Festival, Oct. Magnificent Motors, May Bank Holiday. AEGON International Championships, mid-Jun. Lawn tennis tournament.

Lewes

Artwave, late Aug to mid-Sep. Visual arts festival. Lewes Bonfire Night. Marching bands, flaming torches and huge firework displays at sites all over town, 5 Nov (or 4 Nov).

Newhaven

Battle of Britain day, Sep. Newhaven Fort. Period dress, military vehicles and more.

Tea Rooms

Bill's
Cliffe High Street, Lewes BN7 2AN. Tel: 01273 476918; www.billsproducestore.co.uk
Bill's combines a produce store and a café where you can sample some delicious food, much of it made from fruit and vegetables sold in the shop itself. The salads, quiches and light dishes like eggs Benedict with smoked salmon, plus the popular fruit smoothies, are served all morning and afternoon, alongside daily specials.

Exceat Farmhouse Restaurant
Seven Sisters Country Park BN25 4AD
Tel: 01323 870218
A delightful old farmhouse with bedrooms, offering home-made cakes, teas, light lunches, traditional and continental cuisine. It's set back from the A259, and is perfectly positioned for strolls to Cuckmere Haven or through Friston Forest.

Fusciardi's
30 Marine Parade, Eastbourne BN22 7AY
Tel: 01323 722128
Well-loved Italian family-run gelateria and cappuccino bar on the seafront, Fusciardi's has served generations of visitors with its home-made ice cream which comes in 15 flavours. You'll also find traditional Italian food, salads and paninis on the menu.

Heaven Farm
Furners Green, Uckfield TN22 3RG
Tel: 01825 790226
www.heavenfarm.co.uk
The Stable Tea Rooms here are in beautifully rural surroundings on an 1830s farm just north of Sheffield Park Gardens. Eat inside or at picnic sets on the lawn. The site also includes a nature trail, farm museum, craft shop and unobtrusive camping and caravan site.

Pubs

Cricketers Arms
Berwick BN26 6SP
Tel: 01323 870469
This unrushed and well-run brick-and-flint village pub (near the famous church) attracts plenty of diners, but is also somewhere you can pop in for a drink and enjoy real ale in the low-ceilinged bar. It's appealingly cottagey, and in summer the front garden is a pleasant place to sit, with seats on the lawn amid shrubs and flowers. The menu features hearty pub dishes and they have real ale from the cask.

Giant's Rest
Wilmington BN26 5SQ
Tel: 01323 870207
The 'Giant' is the hill carving in view from the garden of this village pub. It does get busy on Sundays, but it's worth booking for a meal, which might feature local sausages, a range of fish dishes and home-made fruit crumble. There are blazing log fires, pews and puzzles at every table.

The Griffin Inn
Fletching TN22 3SS
Tel: 01825 722890
Very useful if you're visiting Sheffield Park, the Ashdown Forest or the Bluebell Railway. Rooms at this old inn are beamed and panelled, with blazing open fires, and there's a large garden. You can eat very well here, from a menu featuring modern English food.

Rose Cottage Inn
Alciston BN26 6UW
Tel: 01323 870377
This wisteria-hung place has a warren of small rooms, with a terrace outside. Satisfying ploughman's lunches, as well as more ambitious fare using local produce and fresh fish, make it a popular destination for walkers from the Downs.

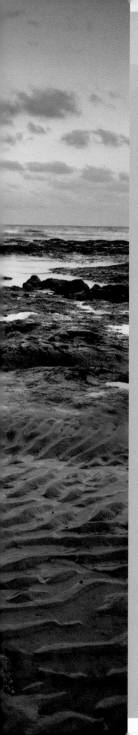

Rye & Hastings

The date 1066 is written all over this area, where the Normans landed, defeated the English at Battle, and changed England forever. The region was fortified and fought over for centuries, and castles such as Bodiam and Pevensey attest to a trouble-stricken past. The old Cinque Ports of Rye, Winchelsea and the Old Town of Hastings have survived centuries of unrest almost miraculously well, each markedly different in character. East of Hastings, rugged sandstone cliffs reach the sea.

3 Cycle start point

BEXHILL

Unmissable attractions

Browse through the antiques shops and cobbled streets of Rye...explore Hastings Old Town, the backdrop for the popular television series *Foyle's War*, and take the cliff railway up to the Country Park...discover the medieval castle within a Roman fort at Pevensey...cycle out from Rye to enjoy the vast beach and sand dunes at Camber Sands...find out that physics really can be fun at the Observatory Science Centre, Herstmonceux...see the Battle of Hastings re-enacted at Battle...celebrate the coming of summer at the Jack in the Green Festival, Hastings...walk, cycle, sail or windsurf at Bewl Water...taste fresh fish bought straight from the beach...watch the sunset from the balcony bar at Bexhill's De La Warr Pavilion.

1 Bodiam Castle
Bodiam, with its four round drum towers, one at each corner, its wide moat and majestic gatehouse, is a fairytale castle.

2 Great Dixter
The colourful gardens at Great Dixter surround a half-timbered medieval hall house that was restored and substantially extended by Edwin Lutyens on behalf of the Lloyd family in 1910.

3 Hastings
The handsome old seaside town of Hastings has a real smack of the sea, with its huddle of streets beneath the cliffs.

4 Camber Sands
The 7 miles (11.3km) of wide golden sands make Camber Sands a popular holiday destination.

5 Fairlight
Spring gorse in bloom on the high sandstone cliffs and heathland in Hastings Country Park, near the village of Fairlight.

BATEMAN'S MAP REF TQ6724

The author and 'poet of Empire' Rudyard Kipling, the first writer to capture the feelings of the British soldier in such verse as the *Barrack-Room Ballads*, was at the height of his fame when he moved into this tall-chimneyed 17th-century country house in 1902. He had wearied of sightseers peering into his previous home in Rottingdean to catch a glimpse of the great man, and needed to recover from the death of his eldest daughter three years before. At Bateman's he found the privacy he wanted for the last 34 years of his life, and during that time penned *Puck of Pook's Hill* (the hill of the title is visible from the house). The cosily dark interior contains many of his relics associated with the Far East, and his study remains very much as it was. He loved being chauffeur-driven along the Sussex lanes, and his Rolls-Royce is on display. It's worth coming here in good weather, as the grounds are a real treat, sloping down to a watermill on the River Dudwell. Adjacent is the pretty village of Burwash, ranged along the ridge, with beautiful tile-hung houses.

BATTLE MAP REF TQ7417

This handsome if traffic-ridden old Wealden town takes its name from the most famous clash of arms in British history – the Battle of Hastings. It took place on 14 October 1066, when William of Normandy defeated Harold and the English. William later atoned for the bloodshed by founding an abbey here, placing the altar supposedly on the very spot where Harold fell.

A visit can be slightly confusing until you realise that the magnificent abbey gatehouse was erected some 300 years after the battle; beyond, the Battle Abbey School takes up part of the site, and by the remains of William's abbey can be seen the more substantial monks' dormitory and common room. To lead you through the story of the battle, the Battle for England exhibition has a film show and interactive displays where you can handle armour and weapons, and an audio tour takes in the battlefield and ruins; in the gatehouse are exhibits about the monks' lives. English Heritage,

■ Insight

THE BATTLE OF HASTINGS

Our knowledge of what happened in 1066 is sketchy – it comes from the Bayeux Tapestry, the great embroidery that shows the events in almost cartoon form, and various pro-Norman written accounts. What is clear is that today's lovely semi-wooded sloping landscape was the setting for a horrific day of struggle and slaughter. Raging from 9am until into the evening, the battle lasted an unusually long time for its period, suggesting that the two sides – thought to have numbered about 7,000 men each – were closely matched in fighting ability. At the bottom of the hill, the Normans were at a disadvantage, but they seem to have worn down the English by attacking, then pretending to retreat, each time tricking a small section of Harold's forces into pursuing them down the hillside into a position where the Normans could encircle and turn on them. By evening Harold was dead – shown in the Bayeux Tapestry hit by an arrow in the eye. It is said that his face was so hacked about that his mistress, Edith Swan-Neck, had to identify him through distinctive marks on his body.

which manages the site, runs a lively series of events here, including an annual re-enactment of the battle. There's a particularly imaginative playground, a hands-on Discovery Room open to families when not being used by educational parties, and a shop with medieval-themed toys and books.

The town itself is full of attractive corners, tea rooms and antiques shops, with three entertaining small museums located just a short stroll away from the abbey. There's the medieval Almonry which contains the the Battle Museum of Local History (including what is thought to be the world's oldest effigy of Guy Fawkes, in a town that celebrates November 5th with great aplomb) and Yesterday's World, which is a delightful nostalgic wallow, with period shops and rooms as well as a display about wartime evacuees.

BEWL WATER MAP REF TQ6733

A real surprise amidthe leafy green countryside on the borders of East Sussex and Kent, Bewl Water is a huge, natural-looking reservoir (completed in 1975) and the largest body of water in southeast England. Rather than detract from the landscape, it actually adds to it – as is confirmed by the huge numbers of visitors who flock here at weekends. You can walk, ride or cycle around any part of the 12.5-mile (20km) perimeter path, which weaves its way through attractive woods and meadows – here and there you cross sunken lanes which until the 1970s led somewhere, but now end abruptly at the water's edge. The waterside Look-Out restaurant makes

■ Activity

ACTIVITIES ON BEWL WATER

Plenty of adrenaline-inducing activities await, and many can be enjoyed by all ages. By the visitor centre is a zip wire (minimum age seven), while on the reservoir one way of getting around is by hydroballing within a gigantic plastic bubble – literally walking on water. Courses and activities led by qualified instructors at Bewl Water Outdoor Centre include kayak canoeing, sailing and powerboating; they have rock-climbing courses on Harrison's Rocks. Bewl Water is rated as one of the region's top spots for trout fishing. Permits, tackle, boat hire and courses are available April to November. Bike hire is available at weekends.

the most of the pleasant views from its conservatory and terrace. Boat trips aboard the *Swallow* cruise the lake during the summer months, weather permitting. The main entrance to Bewl Water is found off the A21, south of Lamberhurst. If you want to reach the water on foot, the village of Ticehurst – on the southern side – makes a very attractive starting point with several paths linking to the lake-shore path.

BEXHILL MAP REF TQ7407

A world-renowed example of Modernist architecture is the surprising seafront centrepiece of this quiet late Victorian and Edwardian seaside town. Here, the recently restored De La Warr Pavilion feels like a generous, calming and welcoming public space embodying the Modernist ideals of bringing light and air to everybody. Designed in 1935 by architects Erich Mendelsohn and Serge

Chermayeff, the Pavilion is earliest building of its kind in Britain (for more on the architecture join one of the building tours that take place twice a month on Sundays). It now sits slightly improbably behind the fancy cupolas and twiddly balustrades of the 1911 Colonnades – the money ran out for a planned Modernist lido to replace them – and next to the Indian-looking Moorish arches and the little turrets of Marina Court Avenue which were influenced by the town's links with the British Empire.

Bexhill's shingle beach has some sand at low tide, and in 1901 became the first mixed bathing beach in Britain. At around this time its seafront hosted the first motor races, and Bexhill still hosts classic car events on the August Bank Holiday. Bexhill Museum, located just inland from the seafront clock tower, displays dinosaur fossils, archaeological finds and some exhibits on the history and growth of the town. The cream of the collection are the exhibits celebrating the town's links with early motor racing (with a Bexhill-built Elva sports racing car proudly on show), and the costume displays, which rotate and include the likes of a tiny dress worn by the infant Winston Churchill and a lady's cycling outfit from the early years

Just uphill from the railway station, Bexhill Old Town has weatherboarded white houses that are typical of the Kent and Sussex Weald. The walled terraces of Manor Gardens slope gently down.

BODIAM CASTLE MAP REF TQ7826

This wonderfully preserved medieval castle perfectly evokes the golden age of chivalry. Surrounded by a water-filled moat full of water lilies and patrolled by elegant swans, the castle's walls and drum towers still rise virtually to their original height. The castle dates from 1385 when Sir Edward Dalyngrigge built it, having fought for Edward III. It was scarcely state of the art in that era of gunpowder, where the trend was soon to build with concentric defences – but Bodiam was never really put to the test. Looking like everyone's idea of a perfect castle, it is an almost unfailing hit with most children: inside there are spiral staircases and battlements to explore, and the lawns around it make an ideal place for picnics. There are children's activity packs, as well as special events organised by the National Trust.

GREAT DIXTER
MAP REF TQ8226

Secretive, enclosed, domestic-scale and capturing the sense of place of the Kent-Sussex Weald, Great Dixter has an enchanted quality from the start, as a flagged path leads you in between wild flower meadows neatly enclosed by yew hedges clipped into blocky geometric shapes.

The hallmark of this garden, the life work of the celebrated garden writer Christopher Lloyd (1921–2006), is its uninhibited use of colour. It feels bigger than it is, full of changes of level and unexpected glimpses, as it dips through narrow arches of topiary to reveal new outdoor 'rooms'. A sunken garden with an octagonal pond is flanked by old barns and oast houses: a huge red-tiled roof slopes down almost to ground level

BEXHILL

and fig trees are trained fan-wise over an entire weather-boarded barn wall.

The planting is dense with masses of contrasting colour and foliage, changing subtly as you descend towards the very extensive nursery at the back, across another wildflower meadow that is full of buttercups, ox-eye daisies, clover and pyramid orchids, and dotted with topiary shapes. Lloyd was well known for his independence when it came to garden design and colour combinations, his vision unshaken by fashions and fads.

HASTINGS MAP REF TQ8209

With fresh fish sold from the beach and gulls wheeling noisily, Hastings has a really maritime feel to it. Its dramatic landscapes, historic survivals and its collection of very individual museums and attractions make it an appealing place to visit. The 20th century was not always kind to the town, and it still feels only half-discovered, but so far the 21st century is proving more appreciative: millions would recognise many Hastings locations from the popular ITV series *Foyle's War*, and its lively pubs and cafés, festivals and atmosphere are attracting students, artists and musicians.

The Old Town is the place where Hastings' independent shops and eating places cluster along the High Street and George Street, a cheerful jumble of old buildings with secondhand dealers and traditional-looking tea shops like Katie's Pantry alongside newer boutiques and café-restaurants. It's worth wandering round at length around the quarters where the fishermen and their families originally lived, up stepped alleys like

Woods Passage. Look out for the tiny Piece of Cheese House found at 10 Starr Cottages (next to 60a All Saints Street). The Old Town Hall Museum in the High Street is set out as a walk back in time from the housing clearances of the 1930s to prehistoric discoveries, and the Shirley Leaf and Petal Company at 58a High Street is a fascinating visit.

The Stade, the pebbly expanse from which Europe's largest beach-launched fishing fleet still operates, is a working area, with winching equipment, rusting tractors, skeletal ship remains, old rope and lobster pots lying around. Near by are the distinctive net shops – tall black-tarred sheds built high and narrow to avoid the land taxes of the time – and a remarkable set of items commemorating maritime traditions and heritage. The Lifeboat Station displays hand-painted panels listing rescues going back to 1863.

The old Fishermen's Church now shelters Hastings' last sailing lugger at the Fishermen's Museum, surrounded by evocative photographs of weatherbeaten, bewhiskered characters and mementoes of the town's fishing history, while the Shipwreck and Coastal Heritage Centre tells the story of local shipwrecks and underwater archaeology. Finds from one Danish ship sunk in 1863 are reassembled within a seabed scene alongside muskets, gin and unopened brandy bottles. Opposite is Hastings Blue Reef Aquarium, with excellent views of native sea creatures, an underwater tunnel and a tropical marine section.

There are two historic cliff railways in Hastings. The East Hill Lift, just by the net shops, will take you to the Hastings Country Park and on to the cliffs. The West Hill Lift runs from George Street to an expanse of sloping lawns, with the ruins of Hastings Castle to one side and the stepped descent back to the Old Town on the other. The viewing terrace of the simple café at the top is a good place to take in the seafront panorama.

Hastings Castle partly crumbled off the edge of the cliff centuries ago. Its remains, close to the site of William the Conqueror's first English castle, are perched high on a mound above the town. There is a lively audio-visual exhibition within the castle grounds about the Battle of Hastings (fought not here, but inland at Battle).

Across West Hill, Smugglers Adventure uses sandstone caves carved out with niches and columns as a setting for tableaux and exhibits on smugglers' tales and ghosts. The history of the caves as a Victorian tourist attraction, a bizarre venue for dances and an air-raid shelter is interesting in itself – look out for the replica prehistoric animal paintings.

Between the old and 'new' (Victorian) town the seafront strip has fish and chip shops and amusement arcades on the landward side, and a boating lake, crazy golf, go-karting, a miniature railway and trampolines opposite. Beyond here, towards the pier, Pelham Beach has flat sands at low tide and lifeguard patrols.

Hastings Museum and Art Gallery, set in the newer part of town west of the railway station has revamped galleries featuring the stories of three very influential Hastings residents. The television pioneer John Logie Baird produced the first shadowy transmission here; Robert Tressell, author of the passionate socialist novel *The Ragged Trousered Philanthropists* based on his experiences of working in the town as a signwriter and decorator before the First World War; and Grey Owl (Archie Belaney), something of a celebrity in the 1930s, who posed as a native Canadian and became an early advocate of nature conservation. The museum's visual glory is the Durbar Hall, originally created for the Indian and Colonial Exhibition of 1886 to evoke an Indian palace.

The newer part of town spreads westwards towards St Leonards and the huge 1930s block of flats known as

■ Visit

KENT AND EAST SUSSEX RAILWAY
You can arrive at Bodiam in style by travelling from Tenterden (in Kent) on a steam train on the Kent and East Sussex Railway. Steam trains puff their way through the countryside along 10.4 miles (16.8km) of track from just outside Tenterden (in Kent) to Bodiam Castle on this preserved section of railway. The line closed in 1961 but enthusiasts reopened a short stretch of it 13 years later, and by 2000 it was extended to Bodiam. There's a loco yard to look round at Rolvenden, and the Colonel Stevens Railway Museum in Tenterden pays homage to the builder of the railway. Rail buffs of all ages have something to savour here: there are Thomas the Tank Engine days for children, and you can learn how to drive a steam train by taking a special course. For more, see www.kesr.org.uk. Tenterden itself is a most appealing destination. Its main street, with its wide grass verges and white weather-boarded houses, looks rather like a New England town.

■ Visit

THE SHIRLEY LEAF AND PETAL COMPANY AND MUSEUM

Brenda Wilson's apparently tiny shop at 58a High Street in Hastings' Old Town conceals a remarkable international operation. Film-makers, opera houses and theatres worldwide rely on the company's artificial leaves and flowers for their sets – it supplied thousands of red rose petals for one of the arena scenes in *Gladiator* (2000). It's the only working example left in Europe of a once-thriving Victorian industry whose products decorated hats, ball gowns, Christmas crackers and perfume bottles. In the basement you can see some of the 10,000 original tools from the family firm Brenda acquired in 1981, alongside exhibits on the social history of flower-making and bales of jewel-coloured velvets dating back to the 1930s.

■ Insight

DOLPHIN SPOTTING

Bottlenose dolphins may be seen along the Sussex coast between Rye Harbour and Bexhill between the months of March and September. Reaching up to 13 feet (4m) long, they are easiest to see in the early morning and late evening, when the tide is high and the water calm.

Marine Court, built in the style of an ocean liner, and the seafront Marina Pavilion. Inland from here, around Maze Hill, are some striking examples of Regency and early Victorian grand houses, from the Classical to the Gothic to the Scottish Baronial, constructed by the Burton family who also designed buildings in Regent Street, Regent's Park and Hyde Park in London.

HASTINGS COUNTRY PARK & FAIRLIGHT MAP REF TQ8712

The stretch of coast between Hastings and Cliff End is unlike anywhere else in southeast England – an area of high, sandstone cliffs with secretive wooded glens (Ecclebourne Glen and Fairlight Glen) and wind-blown acid heathlands that support a great variety of wildlife. Peregrines, fulmars and black redstarts can be glimpsed on the cliffs, and you might even spot bottlenose dolphins and harbour porpoises offshore, perhaps more easily than the naturist beach which is discreetly tucked out of view in rocky Covehurst Bay (access difficult). Rare mosses, lichens, liverworts and invertebrates thrive here, and sightings of stoats and weasels are frequent. The part nearest to Hastings is designated as Hastings Country Park, covering 660 acres (267ha) of ancient woodland, grassland, cliff tops and heathland. The easiest way from Hastings is to take the cliff lift or walk up from the Old Town.

The most rewarding walks here are along the cliffs, but you can use parallel paths to make a circuit. Fairlight itself is a modern residential village.

HERSTMONCEUX CASTLE

MAP REF TQ6411

The science of astronomy provides the link between here, Greenwich and the Canary Islands. The Royal Observatory, established in the reign of Charles II to record the position of the stars to aid navigation for sailors, moved out from Greenwich, London, in 1946, because the light and air pollution was making it too difficult to observe the night sky. For more than 30 years the Herstmonceux Castle estate was the home of British astronomical observations, but it moved its main telescope to the island of La Palma in 1984. The former complex, with its striking domes, is now home to the Observatory Science Centre – a place full of appeal to all ages. It's best to visit on a dry day, as the large-scale interactive exhibits in the adventure playground-like Discovery Park outside are part of the fun, but there's also plenty indoors, with exhibits on optics, medieval machines, time, force and gravity, and more.

Romantic-looking 15th-century Herstmonceux Castle stands in a wide moat, and is the oldest brick building on such a scale in England. Henry VI's Treasurer, Sir Roger Fiennes, modelled it on French chateau designs and it was completed in 1446. Abandoned in the 1700s when the owners stripped it out to build a new mansion, Herstmonceux Place, nearby, it became a picturesque ruin and was restored from 1910. It is now the International Study Centre for Queen's University, Ontario: you can take guided tours inside to see the beautiful courtyard and some of the very modern lecture rooms – these overlook the moat, and have Jacobean panelling, a dungeon with a stone toilet and a resident ghost.

The Elizabethan gardens and grounds move from the formal to the wild, rising gently up from the castle. Within a high brick wall, robust yew hedges enclose rhododendron, rose and herb gardens and a giant tilted steel sundial. Outside the wall, paths lead over rough meadows to a folly, a lily-filled lake and woods known for their carpets of bluebells.

PEVENSEY MAP REF TQ6504

The outer walls of Pevensey Castle enclose a huge oval of grassland. These full-sized walls are late Roman, with some medieval repairs, built about AD 290 to protect a busy port from Saxon raids. You can wander freely through the east gate, near the car park: on the far right you can see where the excavations below ground level revealed the original Roman wall facings.

The medieval castle itself (run by English Heritage) is set within a moat at the centre of the enclosure – William the Conqueror put a fort here in 1066, but what you see today is 13th century. Then the castle would still have been on the coast, surrounded by marshes. The huge stone balls seen around the castle were for medieval catapult machines: the missiles were excavated from the moat, and they bear witness to the efforts of attackers during three sieges.

The castle was abandoned around 1500 after the harbour had silted up. But more than 400 years later it would have been a first defence against a shore invasion in the Second World War: you can see the rooms used by Canadian soldiers inside the towers, and a gun emplacement looks out over the tea rooms. Pevensey's other historic buildings are strung out along the High Street and include Old Mint House Antiques (1342) and the 16th-century Court House museum.

The extensive shingle beach is at Pevensey Bay, about a mile (1.6km) away. To the north are the Pevensey Levels, a reclaimed marsh with reed-fringed ditches, tiny lanes and isolated farms.

A loop from Pevensey to Herstmonceux

A journey between two castles, through the lonely expanse of the Pevensey Levels in '1066 Country'. They may be flat, but the Pevensey Levels are full of colour, character and wildlife, while the South Downs rise dramatically in the background. The ride connects the two contrasting castles at Pevensey and Herstmonceux via a winding, almost traffic-free lane, then a wider road leads down to the village of Wartling and then across the Levels to Pevensey.

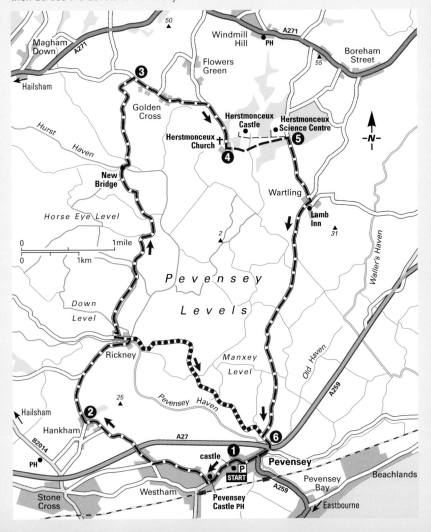

Route Directions

1 From the car park, go to the main street in Pevensey and turn left along it, passing the outer wall of the castle (you can walk in through the gateway, where there is free access, if you don't intend to visit the castle fully later). Just after the Pevensey Castle pub turn right along Peelings Lane, ignoring a minor turn soon on the left. Turn right at a crossroads and follow signs to Hankham.

2 Turn right at a T-junction in Hankham, signposted 'Rickney'. Keep right at the next junction for Rickney (National Cycle Route 2). For a short loop back, at the next junction (in Rickney itself) turn right, then right after 1.5 miles (2.4km). Cross the roundabout and take the road back into Pevensey. To take the main cycle ride, turn left at the junction in Rickney (signposted 'Hailsham'), then take the first right, signposted 'Herstmonceux'. Both the short and full rides afford lovely views across the Pevensey Levels.

3 After 3 miles (4.8km) turn right at the next junction and then keep right at the next two junctions to reach Herstmonceux church; note the mounting block for horse-riders outside. Have a look inside for the tomb of Thomas Lord Dacre (died 1553) and his son Sir Thomas Fiennes.

4 Past the church, where the public road ends, go forward, veering left on the bridleway, and follow blue arrows and waymarkers for the 1066 Country Walk. This leads over a surfaced area near college outbuildings and a car park, and down through woodland (it can be muddy). It then crosses a field, with a view of Herstmonceux Castle to the left; it is not always open to the public, so enjoy the view from here. Ahead is one of the telescope buildings of the former Royal Greenwich Observatory. The observatory, which had to move from Herstmonceux, is now based in the Canary Islands. Push your bike up some steps and later you will see the other domes of the old observatory (now the Herstmonceux Science Centre).

5 Turn right on the road (just to the left is the entrance to the Science Centre and Herstmonceux Castle and grounds) and cycle down to Wartling, keeping right in front of the Lamb Inn. Continue for 2.5 miles (4km) back to the edge of Pevensey.

6 Cross the roundabout carefully, using the cycle crossing points, and take the road into Pevensey to return to the start point.

Route facts

DISTANCE/TIME 13 miles (20.9km) 2h30
Alternative route 5.5 miles (8.8km) 1h

MAP OS Explorer 124: Hastings and Bexhill

START Pevensey car park (by castle; pay and display); grid ref: TQ646048

TRACKS All on minor roads, except for an earthy bridleway at Herstmonceux (well-drained but uneven surface, and stepped for a short distance; necessary to push your bike; the short ride is on roads.

GETTING TO THE START
Pevensey is just west of the A27 and A259 junction, east of Eastbourne.

CYCLE HIRE Seven Sisters Cycle Company, next to Seven Sisters Country Park Visitor Centre, Exceat. Tel: 01323 870310; www.cuckmere-cycle.co.uk

THE PUB The Lamb Inn, Wartling. Tel: 01323 823116; www.lambinnwartling.co.uk

❶ The 0.75 mile (1.2km) off-road section at Herstmonceux may be muddy and includes steps, where you will have to push. Take care on the roundabout outside Pevensey.

◼ Activity

CAMBER SANDS

The best sandy beach in Sussex, Camber Sands is ideal for a family day out, with large dunes and shallow waters (though beware of incoming tides). A short way southeast of Rye, it can be reached by a 3-mile (4.8km) bike path from Rye that runs closely parallel to the road from Rye itself – or by bus from Rye station. There are large car parks with toilets, and a few cafés and shops in Camber village.

◼ Visit

CAMBER CASTLE

Brooding on the low drained marshland 1 mile (1.6km) towards the sea from Rye, Camber Castle is nearer Winchelsea than Camber, and is reached by a footpath across the meadows from Rye or via Rye Harbour nature reserve. The substantial artillery fort was begun in 1512 and enlarged between 1539 and 1544, as part of a chain of defences built by Henry VIII, but its days were short lived, as the sea receded. Unlike other forts of this period it remains unaltered. If it is closed you get a good idea of it by peering in from outside.

RYE MAP REF TQ9221

Rye is a perfectly preserved small medieval hilltop town. Cars wind round the bottom of the slopes: above, the cobbled streets are on an early medieval layout, and many houses date from the 16th and 17th centuries. Mermaid Street, with its eccentric house names and the handsome old Mermaid Inn, is the most photographed spot, but there are lots of other parts to explore. Around Church Square and Watchbell Street no house matches its neighbour, but they combine harmoniously, opening straight onto the cobbles and flagstones. The mostly Norman St Mary's Church has later additions like the Quarter Boys clock (it chimes on the quarter hour) and the elegant oval brick structure of the 18th-century public water cistern in a corner of the churchyard.

Rye scores highly as a place to visit on many counts, particularly for dining and shopping. The antiques shops, craft potteries and bric-à-brac shops are concentrated around the old fishermen's huts near the car park on Strand Quay – a reminder of when the sea came right up to the town – and the Town Model show at the Heritage Centre here is a useful introduction to the town's history. The shops in the High Street combine traditional town shopping with speciality businesses. The Jacobean brick of the old Grammar School (1636) houses a record shop, while Adams Stationers has a collection of old railway signs. The Landgate was at one time the only land entrance to Rye: the pioneering lesbian author Radclyffe Hall lived near here, her house is marked by a plaque.

Lamb House in West Street dates from 1723 and is owned by the National Trust; American author Henry James lived the life of an English gentleman in this Georgian property's gracefully proportioned rooms. He wrote his later works, including *The Wings of the Dove*, *The Ambassadors* and *The Golden Bowl*, in a garden house, demolished by a Second World War air raid. James's friend E F Benson later leased the house, and set his Mapp and Lucia stories in Rye (which he called Tilling).

Local history is on display in the Rye Castle Museum in East Street, with artefacts on the fishing industry and the Rye potteries, and in the 13th-century Ypres Tower which served as the town jail for 400 years. Some of the tiny cells are open, and downstairs there are replica medieval helmets and weapons to try out. Outside in the Gun Garden, a public terrace below the Tower, a row of five cannons aims down the river and there are views over Rye Harbour.

Rye Harbour, a Site of Special Scientific Interest, is one of only a few stable shingle habitats in Europe: warm, open and dry, it is home to birds such as little terns, oystercatchers and curlews, and plants such as yellow horned-poppy and sea kale. It's an atmospheric coastal experience, though you have to get there via the unappealingly industrial Harbour Road by the river (buses from Rye). Beyond the car park a surfaced track leads through saltmarshes and past gravel pits to the nature reserve information centre in Lime Kiln Cottage, and beyond to the river mouth and along the beach. Here the views extend to the golden sandstone cliffs at Fairlight in the west, to Camber Sands (tantalisingly unreachable from here) and the pylons radiating out from Dungeness nuclear power station in the east. The beach itself is shingle with sand at low tide. The information centre has maps, walks and a virtual tour: there are guided walks and hides for birding. Nearby Rye Harbour village has a Watch House, Martello tower, lifeboat station and small boats stranded on mud banks at low tide. It has two pubs and a café.

WINCHELSEA MAP REF TQ9117

Now a peaceful, spread-out village of neat old houses with just a pub, church, tea room and shop, there is little other than the remains of town defences far out in the surrounding fields to hint that Winchelsea once knew greater things. Before a combination of French attacks, the Black Death and the river silting up virtually put paid to its prosperity, it was a thriving port (from 1191 it became one of the royal Cinque Ports), planned by royal command in 1283, and second in the nation as a centre for shipbuilding.

The 13th-century grid plan is obvious wherever you go in Winchelsea's wide straight streets, and it is recognised as a rare English example of one of the medieval fortified 'bastide' towns more common in parts of France. The houses look later though, mostly 17th and 18th century – a handsome blend of brick, weatherboarding and tile-hanging. There are three medieval gateways: Pipewell Gate (by the main road) and Strand Gate (on the cliff edge, with a view towards Rye and Romney Marsh) are in the town while the ruined New Gate spans a lane well outside (follow the 1066 Country Walk south from the village).

Filling an entire square of the grid plan is the early 14th-century Church of St Thomas the Martyr. The French raids destroyed all of it except the chancel and chapels, which form today's church. The flamboyant tracery and the elaborate canopied tombs hint at massive wealth in times past. Opposite the church, there is a model of the medieval town in the Winchelsea Court Hall Museum, which has the former jail on its ground floor.

■ TOURIST INFORMATION CENTRES

Battle
Battle Abbey, High Street.
Tel: 01424 773721;
www.1066country.com

Hastings
Queens Square,
Priory Meadow.
Tel: 01424 451111
The Stade, Old Town.
Tel: 01424 451111;
www.1066country.com

Rye
Rye Heritage Centre,
Strand Quay.
Tel: 01797 226696;
www.visitrye.co.uk

■ PLACES OF INTEREST

BURWASH
Bateman's.
Tel: 01435 882302;
www.nationaltrust.org.uk

HASTINGS
Battle Abbey
Tel: 01424 773792;
www.english-heritage.org.uk

Bodiam Castle
Tel: 01580 830190;
www.nationaltrust.org.uk

Hastings Museum & Art Gallery
Johns Place, Bohemia Road.
Tel: 01424 781155;
www.hmag.org.uk

Shirley Leaf and Petal Museum
58a High Street,
Old Town, Hastings.
Tel: 01424 427793

PEVENSEY
Pevensey Castle
Tel: 01323 762604;
www.english-heritage.org.uk

WINCHELSEA
Winchelsea Court Hall Museum
High Street.
Tel: 01797 224395; www.winchelseamuseum.co.uk

FOR CHILDREN

Clambers Children's Play Centre
White Rock Gardens,
Hastings. Tel: 01424 423778;
www.clambers.co.uk
Both indoor and outdoor
play areas.

Hastings Blue Reef Aquarium
Rock-a-Nore Road, Hastings.
Tel: 01424 718776;
www.bluereefaquarium.co.uk

The Observatory Science Centre
Herstmonceux.
Tel: 01323 832731;
www.the-observatory.org

Smugglers Adventure
St Clements Caves, Hastings.
Tel: 01424 422964; www.smugglersadventure.co.uk

Yesterday's World
Battle. Tel: 01424 775888;
www.yesterdaysworld.co.uk

■ SHOPPING

Rye stands out for its stylish
contemporary shopping, as
well as for its stores selling
collectables and down-to-
earth everyday goods.
Hastings Old Town is a good
place for browsing around in
the many smart galleries and
interesting secondhand
shops. You'll find plenty of
the high street chains in the
town centre.

RYE
Rye Delicatessen
28b High Street.
Tel: 01797 226521
Useful for picnic items.

Ironmongers Extraordinary
1 High Street.
Tel: 01797 222110
Classy cookware.

FARMERS' MARKETS
Battle
Every 3rd Sat of month.

Bexhill
Every 4th Thu of month.

Brede
Every Fri.

Hastings
Every 2nd and 4th Thu
of month.

Rye
Every Wed.

■ PERFORMING ARTS

Bodiam Castle
Tel: 01580 830196;
www.nationaltrust.org.uk
Open-air theatre.

De La Warr Pavilion
Bexhill.
Tel: 01424 229111;
www.dlwp.com
Contemporary arts centre.

Pevensey Castle
Tel: 01323 762604;
www.english-heritage.org.uk
Open-air theatre
performances.
Stables Theatre
The Bourne, Hastings.
Tel: 01424 423221;
www.stables-theatre.co.uk
White Rock Theatre
Hastings.
Tel: 01424 462288 ;
www.whiterocktheatre.org.uk

■ OUTDOOR ACTIVITIES
CYCLING
The towns of Hastings,
Winchelsea and Rye are on
the Sustrans National Cycle
Route network. Free cycle
maps are available from local
Tourist Information Centres
or you can download a route
description sheet from
www.sustrans.com
Cuckmere Cycles
Bewl Water.
Tel: 01892 891446;
www.cuckmere-cycle.co.uk
Bike hire comes with a free
map and plenty of advice.
Routes for all abilities.
Cinque Ports Circuit
A cycle tour taking in
Hastings, Rye and
Winchelsea, part of a series
of rides published in booklet
available from Tourist
Information Centres.
FISHING
Bewl Bridge Fly Fishers.

Tel: 01892 890352; www.
bewlbridgeflyfishers.co.uk
WALKING
The 1066 Country Walk
This waymarked route runs
31 miles (50km) from
Pevensey to Rye via Battle,
over the Pevensey Levels,
past Herstmonceux Castle
and through lush, rolling
countryside. A booklet is
available from Tourist
Information Centres.
WATER SPORTS
Bewl Water
Bewl Valley Sailing Club
Tel: 01892 890930;
www.bewl-valley-sc.org.uk
Bewl Water Canoe Club
Tel: 01892 724059;
www.bewlcanoeclub.co.uk
Bewl Water Outdoor Centre
Tel: 01892 890716;
www.bewlwater.org
Bewl Windsurfing
Tel: 01892 891000;
www.bewlwindsurfing.co.uk
Rye Watersports
Northpoint Water, near
Camber.
Tel: 01797 225238.
Windsurfing and sailing,
tuition and equipment to hire
.

■ ANNUAL EVENTS & CUSTOMS
Battle
Battle of Hastings re-
enactment, mid-Oct.
Hastings
Jack in the Green Festival

Morris Dancing, early May;
www.hastingsjack.co.uk
Old Town carnival week, Aug;
www.1066.net/carnival
Coastal Currents arts festival
(also covers Rye and Bexhill
area) Sep;
www.coastalcurrents.org.uk
Hastings Week – anniversary
of the Battle of Hastings.
Around 2nd week in Oct;
www.1066.net/carnival
Herstmonceux
Medieval Festival,
Herstmonceux Castle, late
Aug; www.herstmonceux.com
Rye
Rye Bay Scallop Festival,
late Feb.
Rye Maritime Festival,
Aug.
Rye Arts Festival, 1st two
weeks in Sep;
www.ryefestival.co.uk
Autumn Taste of Rye, Oct.
Rye Bonfire, 2nd Sat Nov.
Rye Christmas Festival, Dec.

Tea Rooms

Café des Arts

28–29 Robertson Street,
Hastings TN34 1HT
Tel: 01424 721996;
www.cafedesarts.co.uk
With its mellow and attractive
interior scattered with leather
sofas and armchairs, this is
a relaxing retreat just a short
way in from the sea front,
with newspapers left out for
customers and the walls
hung with art works for sale.
It's actually a social
enterprise with a difference,
being run by people with
autism. All food is fresh and
made to order, and service is
cheerful.

De la Warr Pavilion Café and Restaurant

De La Warr Pavilion,
Bexhill TN40 1DP
Tel: 01424 229 119;
www.dlwp.com
On the first floor of the De
La Warr Pavilion, this
café-restaurant has an
ultra-chic setting in one of
the architectural highlights of
the south coast. Its open
balconies and terraces have
terrific views over the sea.
Choose between the daytime
café for lighter fare and the
restaurant offering locally
sourced food and modern
British cuisine at lunchtime
and in the evening.

Fletcher's House Tea Rooms

2 Lion Street, Rye TN31 7LB
Tel: 01797 222227
Teas have been served at this
half-timbered and tiled house
since 1932, so it's very much
a Rye institution (as is Simon
the Pieman, the even older
tea room next door). It hasn't
changed much over the
years, with its oak beams,
open fire, brass and copper
knick-knacks, and blue and
white plates on exposed brick
walls. You can sit inside or in
good weather eat out in the
walled garden. The food is
home-cooked and includes
light meals, snacks, Sussex
cream teas and lunches with
a contemporary feel.

Pubs

Lamb Inn

Wartling BN27 1RY
Tel: 01323 832116;
 www.lambinnwartling.co.uk
At a kink in the road between
Pevensey and Herstmonceux
castles, this country pub is a
cosy place, so if it's not warm
enough to be out on the patio,
relax in front of blazing fires.
The 17th-century bar has a
snug at one end, and there's
a homely lounge to enjoy a
drink before the meal in the
newer restaurant. The
cooking is accomplished,
and booking is advisable.

Mermaid Inn

Mermaid Street, Rye
TN31 7EY. Tel: 01797 223065
www.mermaidinn.com
The most photographed
building in Rye, the half-
timbered Mermaid simply
oozes antiquity. The present
structure dates mainly from
the 15th and 16th centuries,
and ships' timbers were used
to make some of the beams
inside, where you will find
a huge inglenook fireplace.
As well as sandwiches, the
Mermaid has a short bar
menu and more elaborate
fare in the restaurant.

Queen's Head

Parsonage Lane,
Icklesham TN36 4BL
Tel: 01424 814552
www.queenshead.com
Tucked around the back of
the village, this welcoming
tile-hung pub has sweeping
views over the Brede valley
towards Rye. The building
dates from 1632 and has
beamed ceilings, inglenook
fireplaces and church pews,
and there's even reputed to
be a secret passage from
here to the Norman church.
Food comes in generous
portions, with pies, steaks
and grills, and friendly staff
serve farm cider in addition
to a fine selection of very well
kept real ales.

■ WALKS

Visit the county councils' websites for details of day walks and long-distance walks (many of which can be downloaded):
www.hants.gov.uk/walking
www.westsussex.gov.uk
(click on links to Leisure and Tourism, then Walking)
www.eastsussex.gov.uk
(click on links to Leisure and Tourism, then Discover East Sussex, then Walks).

SOUTH DOWNS WAY

100-mile (160km) route for walkers, cyclists and horse-riders from Winchester to Eastbourne;
www.nationaltrail.co.uk

DOWNS LINK

A 37-mile (59 km) level waymarked route open to walkers, horse-riders and cyclists, linking the North Downs Way near Guildford to the South Downs Way at Shoreham.

THE 1066 COUNTRY WALK

Waymarked route running 31 miles (50 km) from Pevensey to Rye via Battle, over the Pevensey Levels, past Herstmonceux Castle and through rolling countryside. Booklet available from Tourist Information Centres.

HANGERS WAY

21 miles (34km) from Alton to Petersfield.
www3.hants.gov.uk/walking

THE WAYFARERS' WALK

72 miles (116km) following old shepherds' tracks between Farnham in Surrey and New Alresford, Hants. This countryside was also the inspiration for Richard Adams' best-selling book *Watership Down*. Five circular walks (from 4 to 6 miles (6.4 to 9.7km long) are signposted from the main route.
www3.hants.gov.uk/walking

■ CYCLING

The South Downs is laced with bridleways, which are open to cyclists, and offer some of the most rewarding mountain biking in England. For on-road cycling, keep to the quieter unclassified roads. Sustrans, which is developing a national cycle network across the country, has set up some routes that are ideal for families, for example the Cuckoo Trail running along a disused railway track near Eastbourne.

SUSTRANS

National Cycle Route network. Cycle maps downloadable from
www.sustrans.org.uk.
Contact: National Cycle Network Centre, 2 Cathedral Square, College Green, Bristol BS1 5DD.
Tel: 0845 113 0065

■ HORSE-RIDING

The South Downs have superb opportunities for horse riding. For a list of accredited stables, contact The British Horse Society, Stoneleigh Deer Park, Kenilworth, Warwickshire CV8 2XZ. Tel: 0844 848 1666;
www.bhs.org.uk

■ PUBLIC TRANSPORT

You don't need a car to sample much of the best of the area. The rail network gets you efficiently around many of the main places in the region, with connections from London to Winchester, Chichester, Arundel, Brighton, Lewes, Eastbourne, Hastings and Rye, and a line running along the Sussex coast that makes it feasible to use one town as a base and visit others by train. You can also take cycles on trains off-peak and at weekends on many services.

Rail travel

Tel: 08457 484950;
www.nationalrail.com

Public transport journey planner

Tel: 0871 200 22 33;
www.traveline.org.uk

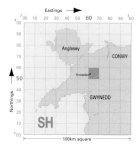

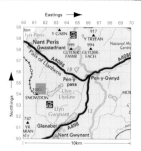

The National Grid system covers Great Britain with an imaginary network of grid squares. Each is 100km square in area and is given a unique alphabetic reference, as shown in the diagram above.

These squares are sub-divided into one hundred 10km squares, identified by vertical lines (eastings) and horizontal lines (northings). The reference for the square a feature is located within is made by adding the numbers of the two lines which cross in the bottom left corner of that square to the alphabetic reference (ignoring the small figures). The easting is quoted first. For example, SH6050.

For a 2-figure reference, the zeros are omitted, giving just SH65. In this book, we use 4-figure references, which allow us to pinpoint the feature more accurately by dividing the 10km square into one hundred 1km squares. These squares are not actually printed on the road atlas but are estimated by eye. The same process is carried out as before, giving an enhanced reference of SH6154.

Key to Atlas

Motorway with number	Toll — Toll	Abbey, cathedral or priory
Motorway service area	Road underconstruction	Aquarium
Motorway toll	Narrow Primary route with passing places	Castle
Motorway junction with and without number	Steep gradient	Cave
Restricted motorway junctions	Railway station and level crossing	Country park
Motorway and junction under construction	Tourist railway	County cricket ground
Primary route single/dual carriageway	National trail	Farm or animal centre
Primary route destinations — BATH	Forest drive	Garden
Roundabout	Heritage coast	Golf course
Distance in miles between symbols	Ferry route	Historic house
Other A Road single/dual carriageway — A1123	Walk start point — 6	Horse racing
B road single/dual carriageway — B2070	Cycle start point — 1	Motor racing
Unclassified road single/dual carriageway	Tour start point — 3	Museum
Road tunnel		Airport
		Heliport
		Windmill
		National Trust property — NT

National Trust for Scotland property — NTS	
Nature reserve	
Other place of interest	
Park and Ride location — P·R	
Picnic site	
Steam centre	
Ski slope natural	
Ski slope artifical	
Tourist Information Centre	
Viewpoint	
Visitor or heritage centre	
Zoological or wildlife collection	
Forest Park	
National Park (England & Wales)	
National Scenic Area (Scotland)	

The Automobile Association would like to thank the following photographers and companies for their assistance in the preparation of this book.

Abbreviations for the picture credits are as follows – (t) top; (b) bottom; (c) centre; (l) left; (r) right; (AA) AA World Travel Library

1 AA/J Miller; 4/5 AA/S & O Mathews; 7 AA/J Miller; 8t AA/J Miller; 8bl AA/ J Miller; 8br AA/ J Miller; 9 AA/P Baker; 10t AA/J Miller; 10b AA/J Miller; 11t AA/ J Miller; 11bl AA/ J Miller; 11br AA/J Miller; 13 AA/M Busselle; 14 AA/S & O Mathews; 18/19 AA/M Moody; 21 AA/M Moody; 22cl AA/D Croucher; 22cr AA/W Voysey; 22b AA/W Voysey; 23t AA/S Day; 23b AA/M Moody; 27 AA/D Forss; 40 AA/M Moody; 42/43 AA/J Miller; 45tl AA/J Miller; 45tr AA/T Souter; 45b AA/J Miller; 46cl AA; 46cr AA/P Brown; 46b AA/T Souter; 47t AA/J Miller; 47c AA/J Miller; 47b AA/M Trelawny; 57 AA/J Miller; 63 AA/P Brown; 72 AA/J Miller; 74/75 AA/J Miller; 77tl AA/J Miller; 77tr AA/W Voysey; 77b AA/J Miller; 78 AA/J Miller; 79t AA/J Miller; 79c AA/J Miller; 79b AA/J Miller; 88 AA/J Miller; 94 AA/J Miller; 96/97 AA/ J Miller; 99 AA/J Miller; 100c AA/J Miller; 100bl AA/D Forss;100br AA/C Coe; 101t AA/J Miller; 101c AA/ J Miller; 101b AA/J Miller; 113 AA/J Miller; 117 AA/J Miller; 121 AA/P Bennett; 128 AA/J Miller; 130/131 AA/J Miller; 133t AA/J Miller; 133b AA/J Miller; 134cl AA/J Miller; 134cr AA/J Miller; 134b AA/J Miller; 135t AA/ J Miller; 135b AA/D Forss; 139 AA/J Miller; 150 AA/J Miller.

Every effort has been made to trace the copyright holders, and we apologise in advance for any accidental errors. We would be happy to apply the corrections in the following edition of this publication.